KIRKUS, LIBRARY JOURNAL,
and THE HOUSTON CHRONICLE
name *The Other Side* one of
the best books of 2014.

KIRKUS calls *The Other Side*
a "modern classic."

LACY JOHNSON bangs on the glass doors of a sleepy local police station in the middle of the night. Her feet are bare; her body is bruised and bloody; U-bolts dangle from her wrists. She has escaped, but not unscathed. *The Other Side* is the haunting account of a first passionate and then abusive relationship; the events leading to Johnson's kidnapping, rape, and imprisonment; her dramatic escape; and her hard-fought struggle to recover. At once thrilling, terrifying, harrowing, and hopeful, *The Other Side* offers more than just a true crime record. In language both stark and poetic, Johnson weaves together a richly personal narrative with police and FBI reports, psychological records, and neurological experiments, delivering a raw and unforgettable story of trauma and transformation.

PRAISE FOR
The Other Side

"In this brilliant memoir, Lacy Johnson offers us a guide to the impossible—how to reconstruct a past when the past itself is shattered, each memory broken into pieces, left rattling around inside us. . . . *The Other Side* bristles with life and energy and to read it is to be transformed."

—NICK FLYNN, author of
Another Bullshit Night in Suck City

"Johnson's strength to free not only her physical self, but also to move through years of incapacitating fear by writing this book, is breathtaking: 'I lift the chain from my neck, over my head, let it rattle to the floor.'"

—KELLE GROOM, author of
I Wore the Ocean in the Shape of a Girl

"Wow. Just . . . Wow. *The Other Side* is the sonic boom of a powerful story meeting an even more powerful storyteller. It's hard to say anything about a book that leaves you this breathless. Lacy Johnson is my new literary hero."

—MAT JOHNSON, author of *PYM*

"This is a forceful memoir of what it really means to survive trauma, to literally live to tell about it. . . . I couldn't put this book down."

—ROBIN ROMM, author of *The Mercy Papers*

The
Other
Side

The Other Side

a memoir
Lacy M. Johnson

Tin House Books
Portland, Oregon & Brooklyn, New York

Published by Tin House Books, Portland, Oregon
and Brooklyn, New York

Distributed to the trade by Publishers Group West, 1700 Fourth St., Berkeley, CA 94710, www.pgw.com

Library of Congress Cataloging-in-Publication Data

Johnson, Lacy M., 1978-
The other side : a memoir / Lacy M. Johnson.
    pages cm
ISBN 978-1-935639-83-1 (paperback)
1. Johnson, Lacy M., 1978- 2. Rape victims—United States—
Biography. 3. Kidnapping victims—United States—Biography. I. Title.
HV6561.J65 2014
362.883092—dc23
[B]

2014006794

Second US edition 2016
Printed in the USA
Interior design by Jakob Vala

www.tinhouse.com

The chimneys of the city breathe, the window sweats,
The children leap in their cots.
The sun blooms, it is a geranium.

The heart has not stopped.

Sylvia Plath, "Mystic"

[one]

I CRASH THROUGH the screen door, arms flailing like two loose propellers, stumbling like a woman on fire: hair and clothes ablaze. Or I do not stumble. I make no noise at all as I open the door with one hand, holding a two-by-four above my head with the other. My feet and legs carry me forward, the rest of my body still, like a statue. Like a ninja. A cartoon.

In the small gravel lot behind the fourplex, I find my car covered by a beige tarp—the elastic cinched between the bumper and the wheels. I wrestle it off and climb inside, coax my key into the ignition. The lizard key chain shakes like an actual trapped animal in my hand, ready to shed its tail and flee. *Take a breath,* I say. *You're not dead yet.*

Inching away from the building, I see the front screen door slapping in the wind against the outer wall. It's too late to get out and close it. The tires spray gravel around the building's unlit side and toward the street, where the streetlights strobe on and on and on along the deserted boulevard stretching between the highway and downtown, where the boys down Jäger shots, the girls down Jäger shots, all of them dry humping at the bar or on the dance floor or in line for the bathroom.

I'll never be one of them again.

. . .

I cross the boulevard by stomping the gas pedal to the floor, fingers ratcheted blue-knuckle tight around the wheel, leaning so far forward my breath fogs the windshield from the inside: proof I'm still alive. Or my breath does not make fog. Does not leave my body, even. Not one nerve-taut muscle gives way as my headlights illuminate the narrow street, the empty parking stalls, the low beige brick buildings.

When I realize I am not being followed I begin to cry and laugh and scream. Like bubbles. Like a peal. The rearview mirror shows my mascara running. Maybe I should apply a coat of lipstick? A patch of blood spreads where I have bitten my lower lip, the taste of a penny stolen from the kitchen jar.

I park the car in front of the police station and run through the dark with my shoes in my hands, cross the cold tile floor—a checkerboard—and pound on the glass separating me from the two female dispatchers, a steel U-bolt still dangling from my wrist. Under the fluorescent lights, their skin flickers black and blue. They lean back in their chairs, hands folded over their soft round bellies, each pair of legs coming together like a V. Their black sweaters. Their blue polyester pants. Their faces turn toward me, their eyebrows raised in disbelief. The clock's arms both point to eleven. They're black. They're blue.

.   .   .

The stationmaster calls a detective out to meet me in the lobby. Tall and wide-shouldered, with brown hair and eyes, The Detective looks vaguely like my uncle: both have kind faces. But The Detective does not smile, does not give me a lung-crushing hug. He leads me into his office with his hand on his gun. Or it is not his office, but an office that is used by him tonight. There is a black rotary telephone with a black spiral cord pushed to the corner of a desk. The wood veneer comes up at the corners, exposing a layer of particleboard underneath. He shuffles in the drawer for a small pad of paper.

Tell me everything, he says. *Start at the beginning.* He does not mean the playground at the preschool with the rainbow bridge. Or the kitten tongue like sandpaper on my cheek. Or the potpourri simmering in the tiny Crock-Pot on the counter next to the jar of pennies in the kitchen. Though any of these could have been a beginning to the story I tell him. I want to see it, the little notepad, but he leaves the room to *make some calls.* No, I can't call my family. No, not any of my friends. Nothing to do but to look at my feet, which are suddenly very very absurd. Someone should cover them with shoes and socks.

He returns to lead me down a dark hallway, where every office is a room with a closed door, through the kitchen, where coffee brews and burns, out a heavy steel door to a parking lot, an unmarked car. A detective's car. He gestures, as if to say, *After you.*

. . .

While waiting in the unmarked car on an unlit street in the dark shadow of an oak tree I realize that real cops are not at all like movie cops. Real cops are slow and fat. Their bellies, in various states of roundness, hang over their waistbands, cinched tight with braided leather belts. They do not converge on buildings with sirens blaring. They do not flash their lights or stand behind the open doors of their squad cars and aim their guns at criminals. These cops, my cops, do not wear uniforms. From the car, where I am sitting alone in the shadow of an oak tree, they look like fat men who have happened to meet on the street, who are walking together around the side of the fourplex toward the gravel parking lot, where they will find a discarded car tarp, a screen door flapping open, all the lights but one turned off.

Just inside the door, they will find a dog collar, construction supplies, and a soundproof room. I have told them what to expect. Meanwhile, waiting alone in the car under the dark shadow of an oak tree I start seeing things: no shadow is just a shadow of an oak tree. I press the heels of my palms hard into my eye sockets, sink lower into the seat. My thoughts grow smaller and race in circles. The adrenaline shakes become convulsions become seizures, become shock. When The Detective returns, he finds me knotted into thirds on the floorboard: hardly like a woman at all.

. . .

At the hospital, The Detective leads me through a set of automatic sliding glass doors, not the main ones that lead to the emergency room, but another set, down the way a bit, special for people like me. He leads me down a fluorescent-lit hallway, directly to an exam room where the overhead lights are turned out. A female officer meets me there, and a social worker, who looks like she might be somebody's grandmother. The Female Officer and The Social Worker team up with a nurse; The Detective disappears without a word. The Female Officer, The Social Worker, and The Nurse ask me to take off my clothes. They unscrew the U-bolt from my wrist. The Female Officer puts these things into a Ziploc bag named EVIDENCE.

Nice to meet you, Evidence.

The Female Officer takes pictures of my wrists and ankles. She speaks in two-syllable sentences: *Oh, dear. Rape kit.*

The Social Worker wants to hold my hand. *No thank you, ma'am.* She is, after all, not my grandmother. Her skin is loose and clammy. She asks what kind of poetry I write as

The Nurse rips out fingerfuls of my pubic hair, spreads my legs and digs inside me with a long, stiff Q-tip. Another Q-tip in my mouth for saliva. She scrapes under my fingernails with a wooden skewer and puts the scum in a plastic vial.

The Social Worker invites me to stay at her house. Or it is not her house, exactly, but a half house for half women like me.

After the exam, The Social Worker gives me a green sweat suit in a brown paper bag. I'm supposed to dress in the bathroom. The clothes are entirely too large: a too-large hunter-green sweatshirt, a pair of too-large hunter-green sweatpants, a pair of too-large beige underwear. Like my mother wears.

The Female Officer doesn't acknowledge that I look ridiculous emerging from the bathroom. She doesn't acknowledge me at all. I know to follow her out the door, to the parking lot, her squad car. I know to hang my head; it's the price for a ticket to the station.

Morning.

The phone call wakes my parents out of bed. Mom answers, her voice is thick, confused. She says nothing for a long time. In the background, Dad gets dressed. Yesterday's change jingles in his pockets. His voice buckles: *Say we're on the way.*

. . .

The Detective follows me in the unmarked car to my new apartment. He offers to come inside, to stand guard at the door, but I don't want him to see that I have no furniture, no food in the fridge, nothing in the pantry, or the linen closet, or on the walls. I ask him to wait outside. I call my boss at the literary magazine where I am an intern and leave a message on the office voice mail: *Hi there. I was kidnapped and raped last night. I won't be coming in today.* I call My Good Friend's cell phone. I call My Older Sister's cell phone.

While I'm in the shower, the apartment phone rings and callers leave messages on the machine: My Good Friend will stay with her boyfriend; she's delaying her move-in date. Of course she hates to do this, but she's just too scared to live here, with me, right now. *You should find somewhere to go,* she says. My Handsome Friend's message says he heard the news from My Good Friend. He's leaving town and doesn't think it's safe to tell me where to find him. The message My Older Sister leaves says she wants me to come stay at her place, which sounds better than sleeping alone in this apartment on the floor.

I pull back the curtains and see my parents standing in the parking lot talking to The Detective. Dad shakes The Detective's outstretched hand. Mom covers her chest with her arms, one hand over her mouth, a large beige purse hanging from her shoulder. She's brought me a peanut butter and jelly sandwich and a snack-size bag of Cool Ranch

Doritos. I'm not hungry, but the thought of wasting her effort makes my stomach turn.

I nibble the chips in the backseat of their car while they take me to buy a cell phone. They want to do something, to take action. With the fluorescent lights of the store, all the papers I must fill out and sign, and the windows wide open behind us, I feel dizzy enough to fall.

·   ·   ·

Driving to My Older Sister's apartment, I watch the road extending behind me in the rearview mirror and try not to fall asleep. The apartment parking lot becomes boulevard, becomes deserted intersection, becomes on-ramp, and interstate. The clusters of redbrick buildings give way to strip malls, to warehouses and truck stops, to XXX bookstores, to cultivated pastures growing in every direction: wheat-stalk brown, tree-bark brown, and corn-silk green.

My Older Sister meets me in the parking lot with tears in her eyes. Her hug is both desperate and safe. As she carries my bag up the stairs she says, *You look like shit.* Under any other circumstances, I'd tell her to fuck off. Today it's a comfort. I do look exactly as I feel.

She isn't able to get off work tonight, so she shows me how to use the cable remote, loads her handgun, puts it in my hand. It's heavier than I would have imagined. She'll work late tonight, but if I need anything, her next-door neighbor, The Sheriff, *knows what happened.* He might come by to check on me. *Please try not to shoot him.*

The whole time she's gone, I watch the closed-circuit channel showing the front gate of her apartment complex. I sit in the dark with the gun in my hand and watch cars drive through the gate. I don't know what I'm watching for, but I keep watching. A gray conversion van looks suspicious. Lights turn in the parking lot, crossing the face of the building. I peer through a crack in the blinds.

I don't eat. I don't sleep.

Even after My Older Sister comes home, offers me a beer, falls asleep with her arm around my body in the bed, I fix my eyes on the dark and wait.

And wait.

And wait.

[two]

SCHRÖDINGER'S FAMOUS THOUGHT experiment instructs us to imagine that a cat is trapped in a steel chamber along with a tiny bit of radioactive substance—so tiny that there is equal probability that one atom of the substance will or will not decay in the course of an hour. If one of the atoms of this substance happens to decay, a device inside the chamber will shatter a small flask of hydrocyanic acid, killing the cat. If it does not decay, the cat survives. It is impossible to know, with certainty, whether the cat is alive or dead at any given moment without looking inside the steel chamber, since there is equal probability of either outcome. And because both outcomes exist in equal probability, this creates a paradox: the cat is both alive *and* dead to the universe outside the chamber. These two outcomes continue to coexist only until someone opens the chamber and looks inside, causing those two possible outcomes to collapse and become one.

. . .

The form itself is simple: my name, the police records I am requesting, the case number, the dollar amount I am willing to pay for copying fees. These fees can be waived if the request in some way serves the public interest. *I was the victim in this case,* I write on the form. *I can think of no way in which this serves the public interest, but I would like to see the files anyway.*

A sergeant in the Public Relations Unit responds to my request within the week. After thirteen years the case remains open and The Sergeant needs to consult with the city legal advisor prior to making a decision, *Since, you know, it involves a serious active case.* Three weeks later, after speaking with the law department as well as the lead investigator, The Sergeant sends me a PDF file along with a polite offer of further assistance.

At first I decide I won't open it while I'm at home—not while there is laundry to be washed and folded, not while there is food to be cooked, and children to be bathed and fed. I'll wait until my trip to upstate New York in early summer. But then I spend whole mornings distracted by possibilities. *Is the cat alive or dead?* After two days, when my children are at school and My Husband is out of town, I open the file, thinking I'll look only a little bit. Just a little. Just a peek.

. . .

The evidence file contains eighty-five pages of police reports, including an inventory of items collected from the crime scene: *chain, brown envelope with handwritten notes, two leather belts tied together,* and *film neg[atives]*. It does not describe whether there are images on those negatives. It does not describe the results of any laboratory tests, or the e-mails or correspondence I sent to or received from The Suspect, though they are mentioned. There are no facsimiles or transcripts of conversations I had with prosecutors or the police. The file does not contain copies of warrants, though it lists the complete set of charges filed on my behalf.

The first half of the document reports the same events during the same time period on the same day, each report from the perspective of a different officer, each report in part relating the story I told to one officer or another. The writers do not reflect. They do not sympathize. They express no pity or outrage or disgust. Each report simply records my story, and yet it is not my story, though it is the same version of the story I would tell. Almost word for word. Like something I memorized long ago and can still perform by heart.

· · ·

And yet, as I read the evidence file, I see things I don't remember. Like how, according to the police reports, it was The Female Officer, not The Detective, who came out to meet me at the station, and The Female Officer also drove me to the apartment I'd escaped, and then to the hospital, and then back to the station. But in my memory, this role is so clearly played by The Detective, the man who looks vaguely like my uncle.

I try to remember my two palms pressed against the glass where the dispatchers sat, the locked beige door to my left. I remember it opening, and I try to see The Female Officer's face instead of The Detective's face. I try to remember her dark-blue uniform, every corner pressed and in its place, the black belt with its gold buckle, the gold buttons, every hair on her head tied back into a neat bun. I can see the long hallway behind her. I can see the little notebook. And the office. And the black telephone. The carpet in the hallway is beige, darker in the middle than where it meets the walls at the edges. But when I try to see The Female Officer instead of The Detective the whole image starts to collapse, and then there is neither a female officer nor a male detective opening the locked beige door. There is no opening the door.

· · ·

Until I looked through the police reports, I didn't know that while I was waiting in the unmarked police car outside the basement apartment, one of the officers called the landlord of the building, a man I knew as the bartender at our favorite dive downtown. He came to the apartment, maybe while I was waiting outside, and confirmed that he owned the building, and that his tenant was a friend, the same person as The Suspect. After The Landlord refused to tell the police where they could find their suspect, and after he tried several times to call his tenant, he was arrested for obstructing a government operation. He was later processed and transported to the county jail.

I also didn't know that, in the early days of the investigation, one of The Suspect's former students showed up at the police department, admitting that The Suspect paid him one hundred dollars to help him build the soundproof room. They spent an entire weekend working on it together. The Landlord of the building let them use his pickup truck to haul supplies and stopped by periodically to check on the progress. At one point he brought fresh watermelon and cantaloupe for them to eat. The student said he remembered that his former instructor had paid for everything with an envelope full of cash.

Until I looked through the police reports, I didn't know that on July 5, the night of the kidnapping, The Suspect called the Mall 4 Theatres, asking if My Handsome Friend was working that evening. My Handsome Friend had told his bosses and fellow employees that some psycho might come to the theaters looking for him, and asked them not to give out any information about him over the phone or in person, or to let on that he still worked at the theater. My Handsome Friend told police that for six months The Suspect had been following him, driving past his house and the building where he worked, because he thought we were having an affair. My Handsome Friend told police he believed that The Suspect might harm him.

I also didn't know that, after the story was reported on the news, people phoned in to the Crime Stoppers hotline to offer information they had about the case. One woman, an employee at a big-box hardware store, had helped The Suspect select glue for the Styrofoam he would later use to build what he called a *sound studio*. One man, who worked at a sound-supply shop on the business loop, said The Suspect had asked him how to build a soundproof room insulated enough to muffle a woman's screams. *For making movies,* The Suspect had said.

· · ·

According to the police reports, bank records reflect that sometime after 5:00 PM on July 5, 2000, The Suspect withdrew $750 from his checking account at an ATM only blocks from the building where I worked. Which means he may have gone to the ATM as early as 5:01 PM, moments before he approached me in the parking lot outside the building where I worked. Or as late as 11:59 PM, after he returned to the apartment where he had built the soundproof room and discovered that I'd escaped.

Early the following morning, before I'd called my parents or returned to my apartment to shower and pack, before The Nurse had finished searching the surfaces and cavities of my body for evidence, he withdrew another $750 from an ATM at a gas station at the intersection of two highways 150 miles away to the west and north by interstate. From that ATM he drove fifty-two miles south and parked his rental car on a street in the downtown business district of one of the few actual cities in the state, where it would be discovered by an officer from the Stolen Auto Division a month later.

On July 7, two days after the kidnapping, he purchased an airline ticket to León, Guanajuato, Mexico, at the Dallas/Fort Worth International Airport. After arriving in Mexico, after passing without incident through immigration and customs, he walked to the ticket desk and purchased an airline ticket to Porlamar, the largest city on the Island of Margarita, just off the coast of Venezuela. He got off the plane in Santiago Mariño Caribbean International Airport that afternoon and withdrew $1200 from an ATM. That evening, just before the bank froze his account, just before I learned to accept the weight of my sister's gun in my hand, one final debit for $29.56 posted to his checking account, from a restaurant at one of the island's resorts.

. . .

One police report describes how, on July 12, one week after the kidnapping, at 9:10 AM, The Suspect called his stepfather at his farm in southern Missouri: a cabin just this side of a shack, the only building I remember now along the gravel road stretching across a heavily wooded hilltop, where it seemed a fresh buck was always swinging from a tree, the red gash of its belly gaping open. I remember eating stewed squirrel in the kitchen at a card table, loading the woodstove in the cramped living room, watching the clouds of my breath from a mattress on the floor in the only bedroom. I don't remember seeing a phone. But it rang three times, the report says, before The Stepfather picked up. He asked, *Where are you?* The Suspect wouldn't say. They talked briefly about the case. *Yes, I did get her,* The Suspect admitted, but he denied the allegations of rape. *If you want to call Lacy, go ahead,* he said. The Stepfather asked again, *Where are you?* The Suspect refused to say, but then started talking to another person near the phone in Spanish. At 10:00 AM on July 12, The Stepfather called The Detective to report the call. He said The Suspect seemed very upset about the media exposure on the case.

.   .   .

In another report, The Detective writes how, on July 17, 2000, twelve days after the kidnapping, he and another officer came to my apartment to talk to me about the case. I told them that The Suspect and I met while I was a student in his Spanish class at the university. I told them that I had been trying to break up with him for some time, for lots of reasons, but mostly because he had raped me on more than one occasion. I told the officers that when I finally did break up with him, six weeks earlier, he did not take it well.

The Detective writes that I told him and the other officer that The Suspect had been arrested before, in Denmark. I remember telling them the version of the story I was told: he was married for years and years to a Danish woman, they had two children together, and after they split up, he took the children to the United States, forgetting to tell her that he was leaving the country. The report doesn't mention how the officers looked at one another when I said this, how they might have wanted to ask more questions about this version of his story but didn't. The Detective writes that I said that The Suspect kept the children in the United States while his ex-wife called and called and eventually convinced him to come home. She told him she wanted to get back together. *A trick*, I told the officers. He was arrested as he got off the plane, and while he awaited trial, his ex-wife flew to the United States to retrieve her children. The Detective writes that I told them that the ex-wife has avoided The Suspect since that time. They have no contact. She gets no child support.

· · ·

The next report in the file describes a fax The Detective received from his liaison at Interpol, who located a record in the Interpol Criminal Register. The Suspect was convicted in Denmark in 1995 of depriving his ex-wife of her parental custody rights and received a suspended sentence of sixty days in prison. Earlier the same year he had been arrested for rape, though the charges were dropped due to lack of evidence. The Detective speculates in his report that the victim in this dropped case was The Suspect's ex-wife, current residence unknown.

. . .

In the final police report, dated August 14, 2000, I am identified as Lacy Johnson: VICTIM. I read this and feel certain it is true. I see myself as the officers saw me: someone who phones the police station to report a suspicious number on her caller ID. I am a subject to be questioned, a story to be investigated, the victim of a set of illegal acts that were perpetrated by a suspect who has disappeared.

And yet, when I close the file, I remember how the truth is more complicated than this. I remember, for example, making choices. I look into his eyes while I undress. When it is done he apologizes and finds me something to eat. I tell him everything is *fine, just fine* and stroke his hair while he cries into my lap. He begs me to come back. Outside, in the hallway, his rifle leans against the wall. At any moment, he may or may not kill me. I remember how the two possibilities can coexist: I'm both alive and dead in every room but this.

[three]

A MINUTE OR two late, the instructor walks into the room and introduces himself. He is not to be called professor or doctor, since he is only a TA in the Department of Romance Languages and Literatures. He is twice the age of his students, at least. A wrinkled t-shirt drapes his round belly, and he often touches or tucks a stray brown curl behind an ear. When he talks, we listen. He talks and talks and talks. He has this way of always talking that keeps us always listening.

The class meets every day, and every day before class I stand outside on the steps, smoking a cigarette, under the awning and out of the snow. Every day the talkative Spanish Teacher says hello, or stops to chat about one thing or another. At first he asks about my major—education or engineering. *I can't decide,* I say. It changes each time I drop out. He asks about my job. What I do in the evenings. He's new here, you see. He asks where I am from. Where I live. With whom. I'm surprised by this attention. And by how he watches me so intently while I speak. The Spanish Teacher talks to me before class, during class, after class. I like his persistence, the way he makes it clear I'm being pursued.

Weeks later, I'm sitting in a dining chair in The Spanish Teacher's living room in an apartment on campus: cinder-block walls painted white, government-issue tile floors, single-pane windows, window-unit air-conditioning. *It passes here for graduate student housing,* he tells me. I don't know why I have come, or why I tracked down his number in the university directory, or why I called and invited myself over. It's a risk to be here, to be seen. He sits across from me at the telephone table, fingering a stack of telephone books, wiping dust from the keys of his state-of-the-art fax machine. The opposite wall is lined with bookshelves constructed of cinder blocks and unfinished plywood boards. I've never heard of most of the titles: academic treatises on socialist utopias in film, or theoretical approaches to translation and international discourse.

Tonight I'm getting the short version of his international life history: an adventure hitchhiking across oceans and continents. It's a far cry from my own life growing up in a town with only three stoplights, a short, failed stint as a model in New York, and a so-far mediocre career as a reluctant college student. By the end of the night he's pulling pictures of his children from a plain white shoe box. Touching them makes him sob like a child. It all starts like this: he offers all that I didn't know I wanted, asks in return for all that I haven't yet learned how to give.

·   ·   ·

I have this image of my parents in an argument, which could occur at any time, on any given day: she sits on the couch like a sullen child—lips pursed, arms crossed—or leans against a wall in the kitchen. She doesn't want to be the first one to walk away from the fight. She's waiting for him to throw his hands wildly into the air, stare at her with his mouth open, sigh, smear one palm across his forehead or push his hair straight up on end. She's betting he'll walk down the hall and close himself behind a door. He talks calmly, deliberately, the giant wheel of his mind rolling her flat. I wish she would speak up, stand firm. Instead, she walks away, gives up, pronounces herself *done.*

·   ·   ·

Mostly my parents avoid one another: Dad in his armchair in the living room watching golf tournaments or reruns of *M*A*S*H*, Mom in her sewing room at the end of the hall, the door closed, her back toward the door, her lap tangled with needles and thread. They spend decades in this stalemate.

The worst of it comes when I'm in middle school, just before My Older Sister moves out. She argues almost constantly with Mom, or if My Older Sister happens to be at work at the town's only ice cream shop, my parents argue about My Older Sister. My Mom says now that may have been what ruined everything, how he never backed her up. My Dad says it was that she never forgave him for anything. Not ever in the thirty-two years they were married. *Not once.*

Before I move out of the house I argue with Mom, too: crossed boundaries, invasions of privacy, unreasonable curfews. One day she finds a pack of cigarettes in my purse and demands I smoke them all in front of her. I break them into pieces and throw them in the trash. She calls me rotten. I call her a bitch and she slaps my open mouth for it. Maybe I deserve it. I think maybe she does, too.

By the time I walk into the classroom that first day of Spanish class, I have moved away from the town with only three stoplights and only one ice cream shop, away from the county with one major intersection, away down the highway to a college town, into an apartment near the mall with My Older Sister. I call home if the car needs repairs. Or if I need to buy an expensive book. I make the hour-long drive to visit on the holidays, but mostly to check on My Younger Sister, a sophomore in the town's only high school. At the end of every visit, I grab my purse and my keys and turn toward the door. My parents hug me, in turns, and say *I love you.* And I smile and say, *I love you, too.*

It never occurs to me to ask for anything more.

. . .

In the apartment I rent with My Older Sister, we stitch together a family and leave out all the arguing. After work we make dinner while roaches scurry across the countertops. After dinner we smoke cigarettes on the balcony and watch mall traffic collect and disperse at stoplights along the boulevard. Each week we change the message on our answering machine: lately we take turns singing Michael Jackson's "Workin' Day and Night" in squeaky falsetto voices. If I am not working at one crappy job or another, I am sitting in a large lecture class at the university, or having sex with boys I barely know: the short one who lives in our building—in his car in the parking lot, on the couch in his living room, and in his roommate's water bed; the customer service manager at the big box store where I work as a lab tech in the Vision Center fucks me in the HR office, the men's bathroom, on the table in the contact lens room. One night I bring home a biker I've met at the bar, who returns the next night and the next, and then he has moved in. On my day off I see an ad for Persian kittens in the classifieds and My Biker Boyfriend drives me to a dark house where I select a black one with long hair from the stacks and stacks of cages. My Older Sister gets a puppy and we all move from the apartment to a duplex with a yard and a garage.

. . .

At the Vision Center I wear protective goggles and feed plastic lenses into the machine, programming precise sizes and shapes on the knobs and dials while music blares from a speaker I've set up in the tiny office at one end of the lab. From the window over the machines, I watch customers checking out at the rows and rows of registers in the main store. The checkers smiling, mouthing the words, *Did you find everything you needed today?*

I bevel the edges of the lenses and dip them into tint or UV coating before screwing them into frames, checking each pair to make sure the axes of the lenses match the prescription, that the distance between the center of each lens corresponds to the distance between the patient's pupils. One of the technicians pokes her head into the lab to let me know a customer needs a contact lens tutorial. I wash my hands and step into the small room, the tiny table spread with lens solution and clean towels, a mirror and tiny cardboard boxes, tiny mouths gaping open: *Oh.*

In the break room at the back of the big box store, I try to call My Biker Boyfriend at his bar downtown. He doesn't answer. I smoke a cigarette and buy a soda out of the machine. The technicians in the Vision Center page me over the intercom to come back to the lab. There's a line out the door. One of the techs is a no-show for her shift. After I check out each customer, I adjust their new glasses to fit. The oil from their skin collects on my fingers and palms. I smile and say *Have a nice day* and return to the register to help the next customer. I look up and see My Spanish Teacher checking out at one of the registers in the main store. He pays and walks to the door. I'm busy, but he waits, watching me. All through the evening rush I feel his eyes on me. *I want to see you again,* he whispers in my ear as I'm counting down the register before close, his hand on my shoulder, my arm, the tips of my fingers.

After locking up, I call the bar again. I am eating a peanut butter and jelly sandwich in the tiny office at one end of the lab, the phone in my hand. Finally My Biker Boyfriend picks up. He was out last night doing coke with his friend, he says. I say, *We need to talk when you get home.* He asks, half joking, if we are breaking up. I haven't decided until just now, until exactly this moment. I clear my throat: *Yes.*

. . .

My Older Sister doesn't understand why I am moving out. My Biker Boyfriend should be the one to go. She and I should stay together. *We're a family.* I need some space, I say. *I need to be alone.* I find a classified ad for a studio in a student slum between downtown and campus, where the rent is $250 a month. I have the security deposit because I have just gotten paid. My Older Sister borrows a friend's pickup truck to help me move my things: a bed, a couch that seats two people, a skillet, a coffee pot, the black Persian kitten and its litter box. I have a few books and CDs and magazines tossed into a laundry basket. She's pissed but hugs me anyway before she climbs into the truck and pulls away.

I spend the whole afternoon putting things in their places. After I drag the bed up the tiny flight of stairs into the raised loft, I use a broom I find in the closet to sweep dead spiders to the center of the brown-carpeted floor while the kitten bats at their carcasses. After I put my skillet into the cupboard and discover an inheritance of plastic cups, I arrange the plastic bottles of shampoo and conditioner in the shower. The kitten drinks water from the toilet. After I make the bed and hang my clothes in the closet, I shower and place a bowl each of cat food and water on the floor. I smoke and pace and look out the windows. I dress again and walk out the door.

. . .

My Spanish Teacher leans against the door frame as I pull into the parking lot, as I climb the concrete stairs to his apartment—his tall, wide frame lit by the glow of the lamp inside. He takes a long swig from a bottleneck beer. I walk past him, through the living room, past the chair and the fax machine, down the hallway, turning lights out as I go. He follows behind me, his hand in my hand. In the bedroom, I take off my coat, unbutton my shirt, my limbs shaking, every hair standing on end. He leans into me. *This is what he wants,* I tell myself, leaning back into him. *This is why I have come.* Because I believe a grown man's rough hands can give, and take from me, what I've lost in coming here. Now my jeans pool around my ankles. *Lie down with me,* I say. Before my teeth shake loose. Before weeds grow from my bones. The unwashed sheets. The open window. His body on top of me: heavy as a pile of stones.

· · ·

It's strange, I think now, how even what the mind forgets, the body remembers. How the body remembers apart from the mind: the way of standing beside or lying-under or sitting-above or rising-from. The body remembers the prepositions: its position in relation to other bodies. The raised shoulders, the lowered voice. How every muscle, even the tongue, can go stiff. Or shudder. How after the other is gone, the body continues on: beside, under, above, from. The shadow, the ghost, the trace. *Habitus:* second nature, a memory so deep the body will always remember.

. . .

We drive sixty miles from his apartment on campus, where I sleep every night, to my parents' home in the town with a one-block business district. They're standing on the front porch when we arrive. They shake hands with him, invite us into the living room, say to us, *Have a seat.* I sit with Mom on the floral-print couch by the front window. My dad sits in a brown recliner by the door. The Man I Live With sits on the edge of the other floral-print couch, in a corner, by the bookshelves, where Mom displays her collection of porcelain dolls. Behind him, pastel pink and blue flowers weave up and down the wallpaper. Mom hung all of it herself before we moved in. I felt ashamed of it then. I feel ashamed of it now as we're making small talk: *Oh, yes, the weather is very unusual this year.*

Maybe it's Mom who comes right out and says she is *frankly shocked* at how old he is: thirty-eight, exactly twice my age. Or maybe she first asks if he colors his hair. Then Dad wants to know if he has accepted Jesus Christ as his Lord and Savior. I cover my face a little and sink deeper into the couch. The Man I Live With answers honestly; he's told me in the car he will not placate *these people.* He delivers a moving lecture on world religions, including an in-depth deconstruction of the savior myth. Or it is not a lecture. Maybe he just waves his hands while telling my father his beliefs are the beliefs of a small-minded man.

During the argument that follows, Mom occasionally chimes in for some jab about this man's morals, his appearance, his age. He jabs back, more forcefully and with a sharper blade. Within the span of an hour, my dad's face has turned three shades of red and he has left the room, close to purple, *fully saturated with the conversation*. Mom cries, sitting next to me on the floral couch. I pick at a thread on the pillow. I do not say a word.

· · ·

The Man I Live With puts our two plates on a little table by the window in the living room of his apartment: tonight it's *pescado a la Veracruzana*. He plugs a CD into the player and we sit down to eat; the kitten jumps onto the table, attracted by the smell of the fish. He is asking about my day, about what I have been reading in my literature class, about what goes through my head while I'm cutting lenses at the Vision Center. I start to answer but then he is telling me about the flaws of capitalism, about how I will quit my job, how I will let him cover our expenses, about seeing Bob Marley in concert in Denmark, one of the last he ever performed. He tells me about the Danish political system and the anarchist camp in the center of Copenhagen. *I'll take you there*, he says. A song comes on, one of his favorites. He puts down his fork, stands up, takes my hand, pulls me up and out of my seat. He holds my hand in his against his chest, his jaw against my forehead, the words in his throat sung so softly. We shuffle in circles from one side of the room to the other, back and forth, over and over, the kitten scarfing down the fish getting cold on our plates. His hand on my back so softly.

He asks if I will love him forever.

. . .

We leave for Mexico during the first week of summer vacation, stopping first in the southern part of the state to visit one of his half brothers, a former air force officer who works now for the Department of Justice. I sit mostly quietly on a lawn chair near the picnic table in the backyard, sipping an iced tea under the shade of a swaying oak tree, while The Man I Live With stands near the grill, his legs spread wide apart. He tells stories to entertain his nephews. He gestures wildly. His voice, his performance, fills the neighborhood.

The next day we drive and drive, stopping only at the Continental Divide. In the photo, I'm squinting into the sun, one hand shading my eyes, the other hanging limply at my side. We descend from the mountains, through the pine trees and spruce trees and juniper trees, into a desert spotted with sagebrush and manzanita, past signs warning drivers not to enter dense smoke, straight to his mother's apartment, where we stop to pick her up and take her out to dinner. *A Spanish place,* he tells me in advance. *Order the fish,* he says, as we scootch into a booth. They speak in Spanish to one another the whole time. I don't need to understand every word to know she doesn't approve. She asks about his children, his ex-wife. Her eyes plead with him from behind her glasses. We stay only one night at her apartment, where we sleep and fuck on her living room floor. *She'll hear us,* I protest. *I need you,* he insists. Or maybe we stay two nights. Or four. Long enough for her to wash our laundry and tell me in her thick accent that my clothes look like tiny children's clothes.

· · ·

Maybe at that time, when she is holding my shorts an arm's length from her body, The Man I Live With has already told me that his mother was unmarried when she got pregnant with him. A young girl away at school in Caracas, knocked up by a Finnish oilman. She came to the United States to give birth, making her son an American citizen. She gave him the last name of his father and took him back to Venezuela to be raised by his grandmother and aunts. Or maybe I don't know this yet. Maybe The Man I Live With tells me this story as we cross the border into Mexico, or while traveling south along the coast. I'm certain he's already told me when we attend a bullfight in the resort town, and when he parades me through the town *mercado* like a prize, because all the next day while we drive down the coastal highway, he keeps bragging about what a good lover he is. *It's in my blood. A birthright,* he says. He says he's seduced women on almost every continent: women in tents and upper bunk beds in hostels. This is how he left Venezuela, he tells me as we approach the resort town, by *hitchhiking in a woman's sleeping bag.* He hitchhiked across Europe this way, across Asia, and back to the States. We check in at the hotel, drop off our luggage, fuck in the shower, and dress for dinner. Before I order he starts telling me how another woman should come live with us. *Would we share her?* I ask, feeling vaguely curious. He explains that she would not be our girlfriend, only his. *You are just not enough.* We'd all be friends eventually, of course. *That's the only way it would work.* By the time he's turning the key to our hotel room, I'm fuming. This isn't part of our deal. *Actually, you're not that great in bed,* I say, emboldened by all the margaritas. *Actually, maybe you should work a bit harder at satisfying me. I've been faking it for months.*

The Man I Live With yells and slams lamps and luggage and furniture around the room. He opens the door and throws my suitcase into the sand. He rips my clothes off and throws them into the hallway. He grabs a fistful of my hair and slams my skull against the bed, holding me there while he spits in my face. He calls me *Puta! Chingada!* He shakes and shakes and shakes me until I am limp and then he storms out the door.

The next morning, he's calmer. He says he'll put me on a plane and send me back home, where I can go on being a stupid fucking hillbilly.

But I have no life back home to return to. I've quit my job at the Vision Center, like he asked. *Focus on your studies,* he said. *I'll cover the expenses.* I can't ask my parents for help. They've said I'm on my own. My Older Sister stopped taking my calls when she learned I never slept a single night in that cheap studio apartment in the student slum between campus and downtown. *You lied to me,* she said before she slammed down the phone. I don't talk to the other students in my classes. I have no money, no belongings, no place to live.

I say I'll do anything to stay with him.

. . .

The Man I Live With tells a good story. In the evenings, after we return from Mexico, he plays bridge and backgammon on his computer and wins nearly every time. Or he plays tennis on the courts at the recreation center and beats men half his age. I love to watch him play: his arms crossing back and forth across his body, his body crossing back and forth across the court, sweat running down his face and chest and back. On the weekends he watches Argentinian films and when I ask who Perón is he explains to me about the Dirty War. He makes beautiful dinners with names I can't pronounce while my cat curls on my lap. We have discovered, after leaving the cat at the university animal hospital all summer during our trip to Mexico, that it has feline leukemia. I consider returning to my job at the Vision Center to pay for a blood transfusion, but The Man I Live With wants me to concentrate on getting good grades in school. He's still sulking about what I said in Mexico, and I believe that if I do what he wants he will forgive me, and then things will go back to the way they were before, when I first moved in, when we would dance around the living room. Instead of skipping class, or showing up late, or a little drunk or a little high or low on drugs, I am the first to arrive in class, coffee in hand, and always have my best work done.

On the weekends, we drive downtown, where the bartender at our favorite dive talks to us from behind the bar and mixes us drinks. Sometimes the bartender's girlfriend is there, too, a veterinarian at the university animal hospital, and she explains to us that, even with the blood transfusions, my cat cannot possibly live much longer with feline leukemia. The band starts playing and we stumble out to the dance floor, standing close together, my head on his shoulder, his chin on my forehead, swaying back and forth very slowly in no relation to the music. He calls me *skat*, a Danish word meaning *pet, darling, treasure*. He asks if I will love him forever.

One night, while we're watching television at home, a Hair Club for Men commercial comes on, and the announcer asks: *Do you have a problem with thinning hair?* And The

Man I Live With says *No,* as if he and the announcer are having a conversation, and we both laugh very hard for a long time, because his hair is absurdly thick and long and curly and not remotely thinning, and his laughter perpetuates my laughter, and my laughter perpetuates his laughter, and when we finally stop laughing, I snuggle into the space between his arm and his chest and we continue watching television.

When the cat finally gets very very sick, we take it to the hospital and it is put to sleep. We wrap its body in a tiny blanket I have knit from fluffy blue yarn and bury it in the yard behind our apartment. The Man I Live With makes a beautiful dinner while I am crying in the bed and when I come out of the room and sit down at the little table by the window in the living room we plan the trip we will take next summer to Europe.

. . .

Even what the mind forgets, the body remembers. I remember the dead cat. The knitted blue blanket. The yard behind our apartment. I remember the sun on my shoulders, the warm black dirt in my hands. I remember crying in the bed. I remember coming out of the room and sitting at the little table by the window in the living room.

I remember sitting, years later, with My Good Friend in her living room, drinking a glass of wine, when her cat draws the warm length of its body under my hand.

Another memory comes back.

I lie in the dark bedroom crying about the cat that has become very ill, about the trip to Europe we will have to cancel because of the cat's terrible illness, about the blood that I have found seeping out of its nose and ears and anus, when I hear from the kitchen a terrible thud, and then another, and another. The thud becomes a crack, a breaking of something that is not fragile. I stop crying and instead listen to the silence that follows, trying to understand what I have heard.

The front door opens and closes.

From the window in the living room I see The Man I Live With walking to the dumpster, carrying something dark and limp in a blue plastic shopping bag. He comes back inside and I ask what he has done. He walks into the kitchen in silence and leaves the apartment with a knife. *Still breathing,* he says, and walks out the door.

I tell people we have put the cat to sleep. I leave a short message on My Older Sister's machine. I call my parents and they say it is for the best. For years I also say this. But, sitting with My Good Friend in her living room, I can't remember how and when I came to believe that lie. I can go back to that dark bedroom. I can close the door and turn out the lights. I can swaddle myself in layers and layers of wrinkled sheets.

My love for the man requires the cat to be living. My fear of him requires the cat to be dead. Each needs and negates the other: the dark bedroom, the warm black dirt in my hands.

[four]

THE THERAPIST'S OFFICE reminds me of an attic in the way the ceiling near the window slants upward, the two sides joining like an A. She keeps a rug on the floor and the overhead lights turned off. A lamp in the corner lights one half of the room, the other half lit by the lamp on her desk, or by the light coming in from the window, depending on the time of day. Two armless chairs face one another in the middle of the room. Like a Beckett play. Behind one chair, her chair, is the desk. Real plants with long, broad-striped leaves fill one corner; in another, an empty birdcage. The Therapist has seen the news. She knows *what happened.* She asks me, in a very quiet voice, to tell her the story again. I tell the story again. At the end of the session, she schedules our next appointment and sends me to the psychiatrist at the student health center. She says she'll call ahead. He'll be expecting me.

The Psychiatrist in the student health center downstairs also asks me to tell the story. He listens without blinking, sitting with his legs crossed at the knees in a chair that could swivel but doesn't. He does not write or move or look away.

I look away. I look away from his thick glasses and look instead at the floor and at my fingers, twisting and picking and scratching at the tips of one another in my lap, and at my feet, which do not sit flat on the floor but dangle off the couch, very far away. *I'm not usually this short,* I say. The fluorescent lights turn my skin green. He asks a few questions: my health, my habits, my dreams. He wants to know whether I use illegal drugs. I lie. *I only remove my head on Tuesdays.* He looks at me over the top of his glasses in a way that waits for me to change my answer.

I tell him almost the whole truth about a set of disturbing dreams. He calls them unconscious ruminations. *Ruminations?* He writes three prescriptions: one for an antiepileptic, which prevents dreams. He does not want me to dream these disturbing dreams. Another prescription for an antidepressant. He explains the mechanisms of serotonin reuptake inhibitors. He wants me to achieve *mental balance.* I laugh out loud. He looks at me again over his glasses. The third prescription is for a very very small dose—he pinches the first finger and thumb of his left hand together—of a different antidepressant, which, when taken in very small doses, also happens to increase appetite. He wants me to eat more. I have to stop losing this weight. He says that while this medication tends to increase an appetite for food it may increase other kinds of physical appetites as well.

He says *other appetites* in a way that winks, though I do not actually see him wink.

. . .

The Psychiatrist tells me to take the blue pill for depression and anxiety and the white pill for lack of appetite. The yellow pill is for forgetting: it puts me to sleep so long without dreaming I forget to wake up. I forget what my name is. I forget where I live.

I know it's the blue pill that makes all the feeling go away because I start taking it first. Or if it is not the blue pill that makes the feeling go away, the feeling goes away around the same time I start taking the blue pill. And by feeling, I mean *feel-like:* I do not feel like getting out of bed. Or like getting dressed, or drinking water, or eating food. I can't keep food down anyway. I do not feel like puking my guts out so I do not eat. I do not feel like going to work. Or like walking alone from my car, across the parking lot, now or ever again. The editor at the literary magazine where I am an intern calls and wants to know where the banner ad is and I say *I'm sorry; I'm a little behind on that. I've had some personal issues lately.* The editor says, *Your issues are not my issues. Get it done today.* Maybe he thinks I'm faking it. Am I faking it? I do not feel like asking this question. Or like being awake. I do not feel like watching television or reading a book. I do not feel like watching the sun come through the blinds. I would rather feel nothing all day.

So I take the white pill, which is supposed to make me hungry again. Mom comes to town to drive me to The

Psychiatrist and spends the whole time worrying that I've gotten too skinny. She cleans my kitchen while I get dressed and after the appointment with The Psychiatrist, where I weigh in at 105 pounds, she drives me to the vitamin store to buy a giant bottle of protein shake mix, and then she takes me to the grocery store to buy whole milk and a bunch of yellow bananas and a big bag of Cool Ranch Doritos and a loaf of bread.

Maybe it is not the white pill, but at the same time I start taking the white pill, I start to *feel-like*. At night I feel like dressing in skimpy clothes—*Look at how skinny I am!*—and I feel like putting on dark eye makeup, so I tell My Good Friend I feel like going dancing. At the club a man comes up behind me and grinds his pelvis against my ass and puts his hand on my stomach and says *This muscle—this one right here—is so sexy.* I push away from him, from his erect penis, and grab My Good Friend and we go running out the door laughing. I feel like spending the night at her boyfriend's house and I feel like sleeping in her boyfriend's roommate's bed. I feel like putting on the roommate's clean running clothes because I don't have any pajamas and I feel like he should fuck me but he just lies very very still.

In the morning there is a message on my voice mail: I've been fired from a job at a veterinary hospital I forgot I had. I pay the electric bill with my credit card and buy groceries with the credit card and when my landlord shows up at the door looking for the rent I get a cash advance from the credit card. I pay the credit card bill with another credit card.

When I start fucking the man who will become My First Husband I tell The Therapist that *things are going very wonderfully* and *I feel all better now, thankyouverymuch,* and I tell The Psychiatrist that I don't need to meet with him anymore, *I'm doing very wonderfully now, thankyouverymuch,* and he smiles and claps his hands together and says *This is wonderful! Just wonderful!* and I laugh out loud because I can't tell if I'm thrilled or terrified by this.

.   .   .

One afternoon the apartment phone rings and I wake up from a yellow pill sleep to answer it. *Lacy, it's me.* Which me? The voice starts explaining how I need to drop the charges. *Sodomy? I didn't fuck you in the ass,* he says. *I know,* I say, the room coming slowly into focus, *but that's what they call it.* He offers to pay my court fees if I withdraw my statement. *The worst that can happen is you'll get in trouble for lying to the police,* he says. Dust motes swirl, the sunlight lynched in the blinds. I wonder how he got this number. It should be unlisted. The bile in my stomach also swirls.

After he tells me he loves me, that he's been shot, that he's lost weight, that he's a new man, he hangs up the phone. I throw up in the toilet and then call The Detective. Within minutes uniformed officers knock on my door. One explains there will be an emergency strap put on my phone, which can be done remotely. No one will be listening in on my conversations, but they'll be able to trace any call I receive. I thank the officers and close the door. I swallow one of the yellow pills before I unplug the apartment phone and drift back to sleep.

· · ·

I am like Superman, he tells me in an e-mail. A reverse search of the IP address confirms that this e-mail, like all the others before it, has come from Venezuela, where he also holds citizenship. The Detective stands behind me, careful not to touch, looking over my shoulder into the computer monitor. He isn't hopeful that the Venezuelan government will cooperate with the extradition, but speaks encouraging words into my ear while I type: *That's it. That will really get him. That's the trick.* In my e-mails back to Venezuela, I play the victim. In my e-mails, The Detective has bullied me into pressing charges against the man I love. *It's the detective's idea,* I write. *He thinks this could be a big case. It might mean a promotion.* In these e-mails, I write that I wish we could still be together. I beg him to come back to rescue me. The police have charged him with kidnapping, felonious restraint, sodomy, and rape. They have frozen his credit cards and his bank accounts. They have flagged his passport, notified the FBI and

Interpol. In these e-mails, we're trying to lure him back into the country so he can be arrested and brought to trial. We're setting a trap: I am the bait.

,   ,   .

Later, back in my new apartment, sitting at the dining table I salvaged from the curb, on a chair I pulled from a dumpster, I hack into his e-mail account. I see all of the e-mails I've sent. He's forwarded every one to his attorney. I see he's applying for jobs in Caracas, and has been corresponding with a South American publisher about a potential memoir deal. One chapter in the proposal is titled "Leather and Lacy"—it's the only chapter in which I will appear.

I change the password of his e-mail before pouring half a bottle of wine down my throat. I take my pills, extras for good measure, and pass out fully clothed in bed.

The next day, the e-mails start coming: each more frantic, more threatening, in turns more bartering, more berating, more abusive. I don't respond and eventually he stops sending them.

,   ,   .

The story is in the paper. It's on the local news once or twice. I never come forward and identify myself as the victim, and without a face to attach to the story, without some culprit to arrest and parade before the cameras, the public loses interest. I don't lose interest. I send a copy of a newspaper article to his ex-wife in Denmark with a message attached: *This happened to me. I thought you should know.* She responds by asking for my number, wants to know if I'd be willing to talk on the phone.

Her voice relates without emotion another version of the events from years earlier: the divorce, the abduction of her children, the trial, and her husband's deportation from Denmark. In her version, she had finally left him after a decade of abuse. In return, he locked her in a basement and fled the country with their children. *You are lucky,* she says, *that he didn't get you pregnant.*

. . .

Rumors begin to surface: a woman claiming to know me personally sends an anonymous e-mail confessing that he came to her door one night asking for sex. It doesn't surprise me. Someone writes to say he once saw The Man I Used to Live With shooting up in the back room of a bar downtown. This seems like a stretch. I never knew him to shoot up, never saw him shoot up, but after all that has happened, I don't know what to believe anymore.

One sunny afternoon The Detective escorts me to our old apartment on campus before it is emptied and its contents are either given away or destroyed. He stands outside the front door while I wander from room to room, touching only the very tops of things. I'm supposed to be looking for my belongings: a silk shawl, some pottery, a textbook or two. Eventually he opens the door: *Everything okay?*

If he comes into the bedroom he will find me sobbing in the closet, my face buried in the hanging clothes.

· · ·

At some point I destroy all the photos of him, but I don't remember how or when. I remember going into the apartment we once shared while The Detective waits outside. I remember looking for the pottery and the jewelry we bought in Mexico. I remember finding an album on one of the shelves in the living room and taking it with me when I leave.

I remember there is a time in my new apartment, after my bed has been delivered, after My Good Friend finally feels safe enough to move in, after there is furniture in the living room and food in the refrigerator, and after there are always empty alcohol bottles on the countertops and dirty dishes in the sink and cigarette butts in empty planters on the balcony, I sit down on the floor of my bedroom and open the album. I shut it again almost instantly. Maybe at that moment I pull out the photos of him and throw them into a trash bag and carry the bag out to the dumpster and heave it in.

I remember there is a time when I have many photos of him—of our two bodies standing in front of the same granite monument, of his face frowning or smiling, of his hand moving blurrily through the frame, of his shirtless belly, his eyes like two bloodshot slits, of one shoulder and the back of his neck—and then suddenly I have none.

For years and years I have none.

And then I find a photo of him buried in an album on his mother's Facebook page—she and I are not actually "friends"—from a trip she took to Venezuela. In the photo, the two of them lean together. She smiles. They are outdoors or near a window. Her caption reads: *My son.* He has changed very little. Maybe he's put on weight. His hair has gone gray. He wears it shorter now. Mostly he looks just as I remember, directly into the camera.

I can't delete the photo, or cut it up, or erase it.

I can't even look away.

. . .

I destroy the photographs of him, but I keep the ones of myself. Even though they're more troubling to look at. There is the one of me sitting on top of the pyramid at Chichen Itza, my bare wrists resting on my bare knees. I'm wearing a gigantic floppy hat and cheap plastic sunglasses like every other gringa tourist in the park that day. Later, as we cross the border from that state to another, border guards will stop us and search our car, one with a machine gun slung over his shoulder, the other with the gun pointed at me, his tongue passing over his lips.

There is the one of me squirting lime onto a raw oyster in Veracruz, my hair bleached white from the sun, my nose and cheeks burned bright red. The next night, after The Man I Live With locks me out of the hotel room, I will stand on the street in my underwear, banging on the door, begging to be let back in.

There is the photo of me standing near the baggage claim at Brussels National Airport, just inside a pair of automatic doors. I'm wearing his blue flannel shirt, my cargo pants, a brand-new pair of hiking boots. I hoist an army ranger backpack over my shoulder and carry a purse in front of my body like an egg. We have just disembarked from a seven-hour overnight transatlantic flight; he slept with his back to me the whole way.

And then there's me nursing a beer from a paper bag in Brussels's Grote Markt, one hand on a knee of the brass statue of Everard 't Serclaes near the square. I smile. I look happy and young and in love.

There's one of me stepping out of the tent at Camping Zeeburg in Amsterdam, cutting through the fog with my long skirt, my face obstructed by a curtain of blond hair. Underneath: a bruise across my cheek.

There's me sitting on the wall of Napoleon's fort in Paris, tired of smiling for the camera.

Me straddling a narrow alleyway in Toledo, one hand and foot against each of the two opposing walls, the flesh between my legs raw and pulsing with pain.

There's one of me buying a shawl from a silk merchant later the same day, my back to the camera.

And the one of me looking out the window of the train between Prague and Berlin, watching the towns pass, the trees pass—the leaves just a blur of green—realizing even then what he's captured in this photograph of me.

[five]

HOW IS IT possible to reclaim the body when it's visible only in a mirror? A reflection of the body, external and reversed: the image both belongs to me and doesn't. The photos, which I still have tucked away in the plastic sleeves of leather albums, reflect something more than what they show: a gaze that follows across the distances of continents and years. I can move my body through the world, and yet there is also an image of my body that resembles in every way the real thing: two people, bound together by this perceived resemblance—a woman who has died, a woman who goes on living.

.   .   .

In the photos of me at ten, eight, and two, there's the long blond hair falling in ringlets, the wide easy smile, the dimple on each rosy cheek. At seven, I am entered into a beauty pageant by my parents, my mother's idea, an excuse to squeeze me into puffy Easter-colored dresses, to fuss and fuss over my hair and makeup. In the pictures, I don't look like a child

of seven. I walk in that sashaying pageanty way I've learned
from watching Miss America on television—I've practiced in
the hallway of our house for hours, for days—back and forth
across the stage, back and forth in front of the audience, the
judges, all of them veiled in shadow, only their smiles visible.

When I go from being a beautiful child to a beautiful young
woman, men compliment my body all the time: the crossing
guard tells me I look lovely on my way to school; a classmate
comments on my budding breasts; a teacher takes note of my
flattering new haircut; a supervisor at the grocery store where
I work compliments my thigh-grazing skirt; my regular customers offer me cash tips, phone numbers, fake proposals of
marriage. I blush, or giggle, or smile at all this attention.

I would give anything to keep getting it.

· · ·

At first I get tattoos as a late-teenage rebellion. On my eigh-
teenth birthday, Mom calls us at the apartment I share with
My Older Sister and tells us she has breast cancer. The next
day, My Older Sister and I drive to the tattoo shop downtown.
We each pick a design from the wall. She picks a rose; I pick
an abstract symbol resembling both a tulip and the female
reproductive system. We each sign a release. We each sit down
in a chair. In the morning, we drive to the hospital, where the
rest of our family—Dad, My Younger Sister, our aunts and
uncles and cousins and grandparents—holds hands in a circle

around Mom and prays. Then the nurse comes, the doctor comes. My Dad leans down, presses his lips to my Mom's lips. It's the first time I've ever seen them kiss. The doctor says a few reassuring words before wheeling Mom away.

I get a second tattoo a few months after the first: a compass centered just above my pubic hair. There is no occasion, really. It's just a thing I want: something tiny and easily concealed. My Biker Boyfriend kisses it each time he goes down on me.

Soon after, I pierce my belly button and start wearing crop tops to show it off. I watch men watch me walking down the street. Months later, I get a third tattoo: the silhouette of a fire-breathing dragon near my ankle. I pierce my tongue and roll the stud around in my mouth while I sit in class. My Biker Boyfriend says it makes me look *kinky.*

Mom says I look like a freak. We're sitting in a restaurant. She has come to town for a checkup with her oncologist. She says nothing about her cancer except that she is lucky: no chemo, no radiation. She sees my tongue piercing and grabs her purse, her hands shaking. *A damn freak.* She stands, the food on her plate uneaten, and leaves.

. . .

A year later, before I think of taking a Spanish class, my parents have stopped speaking to me and My Older Sister. I don't want to ask them for money anymore, so I work as a stripper to pay for my next semester's tuition. It's not hard work, and I don't actually feel all that slimy about doing it. In many ways, it's the kind of job a girl like me has spent her whole life training for: there's the makeup and the costume and the hair, there's the stage and the way of coiling and uncoiling my body until at least one man wants to fuck me enough that he gives me all his money.

I make a lot of money at the strip club, and on my nights off I get free drinks at My Biker Boyfriend's bar downtown. But when a group of boys from my high school come into the club, I hide in the DJ booth until the bouncers agree to ask them to leave. At the end of my shift, the owner of the club pulls me aside and suggests that this might not actually be the right job for me.

I decide to take a semester off from college, and use my tuition money to buy a bus ticket to New York, where I get a contract with a modeling agency. I spend the whole summer sleeping on other people's couches, in other people's bathtubs, on a chair in the corner of a living room. One night I sleep on a roof. Men take my picture and sometimes give me money. They ask me to take off my clothes and then they take my picture. They call it art. They call it *nude*. More often the men call me nothing at all, but instead offer me a line of blow or ask for a hand job in the bathroom before or after the shoot. My agent, a woman, suggests I wear higher heels, pull my hair back, maybe get a boob job.

Sometimes the photographers drive me and at least two other models to the Hamptons, where someone hands us each a pill when we walk into the party and on every table girls are dancing with their shirts off. If we stay in the city, the photographers take us to a new club opening in some once-unsavory district. We don't pay to get in. We don't pay for our drinks and no one checks our IDs. The doorman opens the red velvet rope and a man in a black jacket herds us through the crowd, up to the stage, to the VIP section, where the club owners keep sending us bottles and bottles of vodka. The party promoters come by to check on us and one keeps trying to finger me on stage.

Everyone in the club gets to see.

· · ·

That image, of the self, does not belong equally to everyone. As a woman, I must keep myself under constant surveillance: how do I look as I rise from the bed, and while I walk through the store buying groceries, and while I run with the dog in the park? From childhood I was taught to survey and police and maintain my image continually, and in this role—as both surveyor and the image that is surveyed—I learned to see myself as others see me: as an object to be viewed and evaluated, a sight.

· · ·

When I leave New York and return to the duplex I share with My Older Sister and My Biker Boyfriend, to the Vision Center in the big box store, to the large lecture classes at the university, I start wearing a black leather dog collar. I don't wear it to school or while cutting lenses at the Vision Center. Not while watching *Oprah* on a Tuesday afternoon. Just while I am out drinking or dancing with my friends. Dressed in all black—black jeans, black leather jacket, black boots— I fit right in at the divey basement dance club downtown, where goth kids drink cheap vodka and watch themselves in the mirrored walls. We're all underage, but I'm the one dating the biker from New Jersey who has an in with every bartender in town. At night, I take him back to our duplex and cuff both of his hands to the headboard of the bed. I pull his pants off and whip his stomach with a leather cat o' nine tails while I sit naked on top of him, just out of reach. I clamp his nipples and pinch the skin on his balls. How long do I torture him each night, his cock rock-hard? Half an hour. An hour, maybe, before he breaks out of the handcuffs, or the rope, or the bungee cords I've used to bind him to the bed or the dresser or the stack of metal shelves in the garage. He breaks free and chases me down the hall, through the living room or the kitchen, up or down the stairs—we're both laughing; I'm not really trying to get away—before he catches me, throws me down on the floor face first, and thrusts straight in. I cry out each time in pain or mock pain.

Months later I leave My Biker Boyfriend for My Spanish Teacher. It's sudden and it's not exactly for or about sex, though I give him whatever he wants, whenever he wants it: upon waking, after lunch on the weekends, midafternoon when he or I return from class, and in the evening after dinner or before bed. I want him to love me. Even in the beginning it doesn't work: he tells me to sit up straighter, cross my legs, spread them farther apart. He tells me how to undress. He tells me when to talk, what to say, but he doesn't actually listen. If I hesitate or resist, he takes what he wants anyway. He holds me down while I scream and beg him to stop. I cry out in real pain. This is how he sees me: a mirror that reflects his power always.

. . .

In our apartment there is only one bathroom. The only mirror we have hangs over the sink. It's easy to avoid. I never see my own eyes looking swollen and puffy. I almost never see the bruises, all the tender openings he's bloodied. When I meet My Older Sister for coffee, the first time I've seen her in months, she says I must be trying very hard to look ugly. Which is certainly not, I think, the kind of person I meant to become.

. . .

To celebrate our first anniversary, My First Husband and I get matching tattoos: a Celtic knot he puts on the fatty part of his arm, near his shoulder; I put the knot on my back, between my shoulder blades, where I can't see it. Sometimes I forget it's there.

When we divorce a year later, I tattoo three flowers on my right ankle. I see them every time I shave my legs, or tie my shoes, or pull my legs up under my body on the couch, in the apartment where I live alone.

After I move in with the man who will become the father of my children, I get a full back piece: lilies, lilacs, and daisies cascading from one shoulder to the opposite hip; and a prayer in a language I don't read or speak because I want to keep it private, secret. When it is finished, I start a half sleeve of autumn leaves. Which becomes a full sleeve: an owl, a tree. I pierce my nose, take out the tongue piercing. I take out the nose ring. I start another sleeve.

Now, old ladies in the supermarket stare and stare at me, holding up traffic at the meat counter, their mouths hanging open. They see me, my tattoos, my beautiful, well-fed children, and can't process. Old men say things like *Why would you go and ruin yourself like that?* They shake their heads. They say, *You would be so pretty if you got those removed.*

. . .

When I ask Dad to watch the kids while I get tattooed, he prays about it for a few days before saying no. He says tattoos are not part of his belief system. He says he knows it probably has something to do with *what happened.* He knows this but says no anyway. I stand in the hallway while we're talking on the phone, passing and repassing a pair of mirrored sliding doors, packing my bags for our upcoming trip back home. I watch the reflection of myself talking to him, trying to explain. He's a thousand miles away.

. . .

Sometimes I feel like a very small person. Like I barely fit around the space of a breath. I don't speak because I think no one will hear me. I rarely leave the house. Or if I do leave the house, I wear disguises: long hair, sensible clothes, a pretty, fresh-faced mask. I'm disturbed by the sight of my own naked body. I want to cover the bruises on my stomach and pelvis and back.

Not all of them are imaginary.

I think sometimes about running away. As when I drive anywhere on the highway and it would be so easy just to keep going. It would be easy to change my name. Easier to drive off a bridge or headfirst into an eighteen-wheeler.

Sometimes I imagine cutting myself open to look inside, to dig around for the coldest, hardest, pulsing mass and swallow it whole. I want to take it like a pill and let it dissolve inside me. Or smuggle it across the border—any border—and shit it out in the street.

I want to stitch myself shut.

DO NOT ENTER. CLOSED INDEFINITELY FOR REPAIRS.

. . .

I enter the room at the back of the building and find him ready for me: capfuls of black, yellow, blue, and red ink, blue sterile tape on the lamp and tattoo gun, Vaseline and paper towels spread out and ready to go. A padded black bench waits for my weight, towels and pillows in place.

He tells me to lie down. Or to lie back. To pull up my sleeve. Take off my shirt. Unbutton my pants. To lie still.

Ready? he asks, his foot testing the pedal.

I nod once and then the needle enters and passes over my skin, leaving a thick black line. The layers and layers of tissue are injected with pigment, absorb the pigment, disperse the pigment down and down and down through the damage that does in fact bleed: the endorphins releasing strength enough for me to run, to jump, to burst through walls if necessary. My heart, my breath: in my chest, as they should be, slowing by the end, exhausted.

And afterward, when I go home to wash and look in the mirror, I feel the mark in all its swollen fullness: raw and exposed and seeping. My hands shake as I turn on the faucet. I shiver pulling off my shirt. I look at the reflection.

It both belongs to me and doesn't. A play of light in the mirror. *This is not my body,* I think, feeling dizzy. But then something in me wobbles, collapses, shifts.

I can feel this body: static, living. Not a surface, but an opening.

[six]

AT OUR FIRST session, The Newest Therapist asks me to write two lists: one that describes every terrible thing The Man I Used to Live With ever did, another that describes each thing he ever did that made me feel special and loved. I start to panic. I make excuses. I say, *I have a lot on my plate right now.* She doesn't fall for it. She points to the door, says only, *Write.*

Somehow, the terrible list is easier to start: how he kidnapped and raped me, how he murdered my cat in our kitchen, how he threatened to abandon me in foreign countries. It's harder to write about how he saved me from getting crushed by a surge of people rushing the stage at a concert. How he dragged me to the outer edge of the crowd, his arm around my chest. *We watched the rest of the show at the crowd's perimeter, his arm around my shoulder.*

It's easy to write about the argument we had while traveling in Spain, how he shook and shook me by my shoulders until I wound myself into a tight ball. He left and didn't come back until I was asleep. *He lifted me from the bed so gently, so lovingly, it seemed. I thought he was going to apolo-gize. Instead, he put me on the floor.* I remember it so clearly: the fluff of hair under the bed, the cold seams of the parquet.

It's easy to write that I'm afraid of him.

It's harder to write that he taught me about film, and cooking, and to admit that I'm probably a writer because of him, because of all that happened.

It's hard to admit that I loved him.

When I give The Newest Therapist the list—not two lists but one—she does not put it in my folder like I expect. She puts on her glasses and reads. Occasionally she sighs, or shakes her head. I have nothing to do with my hands, or my face, or my feet. Panic washes over me. Eventually she looks up, her eyebrows slightly raised, as if expectant. She says nothing. She waits and waits for me to speak.

It's possible I'm not remembering right, I finally mutter, my hands in my lap, my head pointed in the general direc-tion of the floor.

She laughs out loud, puts down the list. She asks, *Is there any other way of remembering?*

. . .

I remember how a late spring rain darkens the tarmac as we board the plane for Europe: a smell like dirt, like exhaust, like grass and engine fumes. I hold his hand and lean into his shoulder as the plane accelerates down the runway, tires spinning across the level earth, lurching into that curved space between longitudes, where at first we do not sleep but turn and rock and slouch across the aisle, our heads bent together or apart; and of all the voices droning on across the ocean his grows the most tender and cruel. I remember a blanket, a swirling indigo scarf, news of a typhoon. When someone leans over the seatback and whispers a question, like an aunt in my ear, I remember admitting to nothing but being an odd pair.

. . .

Odd, too, how cool the hour we shuffle from the plane into the fog-filled Belgian city, too early for the black knot of streetcars and taxicabs, no one in their native streets at all except four women in hairnets outside the *boulangerie*, cigarettes leaning out the windows of their open mouths, curtained by the sweet bread-tobacco scent, gossip in an unwelcoming tongue. And odd how our pair weaves and unweaves itself through the stone-gray monuments toward separate beds in a rented room: *Too tired,* I tell him over my shoulder, *for that now.* It doesn't matter. My eyes don't close for hours that night— a surprise concert of fireworks washing the Grote Markt walls in audible light: too loud, too bright for sleeping. The shadows of anonymous bodies dance across our wall like marionettes, each one dangles over the great crack that branches from the floor to the ceiling of our room in the hostel, and surely beyond: the bond between earth and edifice, brick and mortar, history and memory loosening, sliding, suddenly giving way. And like that: anything can be broken.

. . .

I remember how a scrubbed-clean body can rise like new in the morning. I remember how to pack and repack a bag. I remember how to blame myself for almost anything at all as I watch cities pass, stations pass, rail-side tenements pass: brown, rust-brown, gray-brown; blue unshining windows shuttered against the mist-gray sky. I remember how to share a seat on a train with a man whose touch might make me shudder or wince, who often dozes with his head against the window or takes my photograph while I read a book. I remember how we sit behind a commuter in a wool-blend suit, across from two students playing cards. At the front of the car, there's a young mother tucking a curl into her infant's navy-striped cap. Her husband, I imagine, is young and smiling and kind. From my place in the train car I can see how, even on a morning like this, clean sheets hang to dry between the buildings on clotheslines: the white squares bleached bright as beacons.

. . .

We ride the train to Amsterdam, where we pitch our tent at a campground on an island in the IJmeer. At the campground bar, I let a Scottish day laborer buy me a beer. He's as old as my father, at least, and I'm trying hard to understand what he is saying, the music playing loudly, when I look up and see The Man I Live With crossing the bar, re turning from the bathroom outside. He places my beer on the bar and leads me by my arm back to the tent, pushing me through the door, face first into the ground, my cheek hitting a rock under the tent floor, his hands inside me, his whole body inside me.

In the morning, chickens peck at grass blades, pause to rearrange their feathers. Goats take turns bleating in their pens. Cool lake water laps at the campground shore. The thin metal tab of a zipper, pinched and led in silence along its tracks, bobs in the wake of a head emerging from the tent before dawn. Wrapping itself tight in an unraveling sweater, the heavy skirt shuffles along the gravel pathway, through the fog and early light of morning—campers in their sleeping bags still snoring—toward the shower house, like every other shower house, where steam rises thickly out of faucets, the concrete floor darkened by decades of all that disappears down a drain; this naked body like every other naked body: dark or pale, bruised or ruddy, wet and slouching toward oblivion.

· · ·

We ride the train to Paris. We ride the train to Spain. We swim in the ocean and listen to music over glasses of wine. We ride the train to Austria, where the blue bruise of a boat ferries us across a mountain lake. We eat lunch on a balcony, and he takes a photograph of the snow on the mountaintops. I wear a scarf. I lose the scarf.

We ride the train to Budapest, where we share a room at the hostel with three Australian rugby players who take turns touching my breasts. I can't remember their names. Does one have a mole on his cheek? The Man I Live With holds up my shirt for them, pinning back my arms. He laughs without smiling, his mouth wide open.

Or maybe he is waiting in the hall for the bathroom. Maybe he is drawing me a bath. I want to remember being drunk. I want to be standing on the bed, holding my own shirt up, my own arms back. I want to remember that I begged them to touch me. Not how they finally turned away.

. . .

We ride the train toward Slovakia. But the engine stops at the border, stops moving for hours, while uniformed guards move up and down the train cars making everyone stand. Two guards carrying machine guns question a young family: a young mother, a young father, a daughter who whimpers, an infant who wails. No one understands. Other passengers close their eyes, one empties his pockets: passports, tickets.

This is my documentation, Herr Schaffner. Do not refute who I am! Coins clatter to the floor and roll under the seats. All the exits are blocked. We remain sitting and do not whisper. I try to look like I belong with him. Like we belong here, together.

. . .

Earlier in the day I wander into a musty bookstore near the station. It's one of those shops a person can get lost in forever: a leather armchair in the corner and coffee rings on the ancient library table near the register. I find a copy of *Leaves of Grass*, and feel elated to see English in print. Whitman writes:

> The earth, that is sufficient,
> I do not want the constellations any nearer,
> I know they are very well where they are,
> I know they suffice for those who belong to them.
>
> (Still here I carry my old delicious burdens,
> I carry them, men and women, I carry them with me
>   wherever I go,
> I swear it is impossible for me to get rid of them,
> I am fill'd with them, and I will fill them in return.)

I realize, as I'm squatting in the musty bookstore, my back to The Man I Live With, that even if I stand and walk out the door, even if I leave right now and never see him again, unless I come down with amnesia, which happens only on daytime television, I'll always carry him with me. I can't will myself to forget his voice, his face, the rough impression of his palm on my hip's still-forming curve.

The fact is, The Man I Live With will remember the hostel in Budapest. And the train. And the bruise-blue boat. He will remember the campground in Amsterdam.

And he will remember them differently.

I close the book and place it on the shelf, trying not to think about that fact, because thinking about it would mean acknowledging that my story is not the only story. And there is no story in which this, or our life together, makes sense.

And yet it's the only thing I will always carry with me.

. . .

We ride the train to Denmark, where he will stay for a month after I return to the States. While I begin summer classes, he'll stay with one of his ex-wives—not the mother of his children, but the one he married only for the visa—while he tries to arrange visits with his daughters and sons. Before I catch the train for the airport we all have lunch together. They talk to one another in Danish. She glares at me over her plate while she eats her sandwich with a knife and fork, though her mouth smiles and says *It's very nice to meet you. It's nice to finally meet you.* I pick up my sandwich and eat it with both hands, setting it down again to take a long, slow swig from my beer. I say *shit* and *fuck* and wipe my hands on the legs of my jeans. He puts his hand over hers when she looks far down the street.

. . .

Rain falls in sheets between the train and the platform. He pulls me close, roughly—the last time, I tell myself—and puts his mouth over mine, then places several crumpled bills in my shivering hand. I stuff them in my pocket and bolt down the stairs and across the platform, shouldering my way past faceless passengers, into the train cars about to pull away on the tracks. I can't remember the city: the buildings, the streets, all stamped out by darkness. But I remember the way back to the room with the cracked wall near the Grote Markt, the single bed, how I can't sleep with the sound of a guitar played badly in the courtyard, with all the tuneless but joyful singing. I dress and descend the stairs, find a group of backpackers my own age. They introduce themselves and I immediately forget their names. They hand me a cold beer, a lit cigarette. Their open faces also lit. I remember it is morning as the plane lifts from the continent. Somehow still morning when it lands.

. . .

Alone in our apartment, I open all the windows and realize only as the sunshine comes pouring in just how dark our rooms have always been. I ride my bike to class each morning, and to the coffee shop each afternoon, where I recognize a student from one of my classes. We sit together every day, both of us writing. He is my age, and handsome, I think, and he never touches me, not once, though he sits right next to me for hours every day. In the evenings I go back to the apartment and keep writing, writing. I write papers about folklore in reggae and the Jamaican struggle for independence, and about heteronormativity in contemporary fiction, and poems about the rain-pocked creek bed on my grandmother's farm and e-mails to graduate programs in creative writing to request application materials. I call My Handsome Friend and we plan to go see a movie together, just as friends. And My Handsome Friend invites his friends, a couple, and we all sneak into the theater where he works and stay out so late, and instead of crushing my face into the ground or pushing me to the floor, they laugh at my jokes and say, *Let's do this again.*

. . .

When The Man I Live With returns from Denmark we go back to our normal life. I take classes; he teaches. Once a month he plays poker with his former students and comes home with all their money. When he's gone, I apply to grad schools, the Peace Corps, any excuse to move away. I tell myself I will leave him at the end of the year. I plan exactly what to say. When he's home, he wants to fuck: in the morning, at lunchtime, after school, before bed. If I say no, or turn away, or if I find some reason to be out of the house all day, we're up until three in the morning, him screaming at me the whole time, twisting my words until they tell a story I've never heard before, until I doubt myself, until I finally give in, and let him fuck me while I sob face-first into my pillow. Our polite Asian neighbors never complain, never look me in the eye.

. . .

On my twenty-first birthday, he makes me breakfast in bed and pulls a giant package from the top shelf of the bedroom closet: a down duvet he bought in Denmark; he's been hiding it all this time. That night, we go out to a comedy club with a group of his former students, and afterward we go out dancing. In the car on the way home, I roll the window down, close my eyes, and let the wind blow my hair into my face. I'm a little drunk and feeling happy and I reach over to rest my hand on his leg. I feel his hand in my hair so softly, his fingers rubbing the back of my head so softly, his hand pulling me toward him, toward his lap, pushing me down, down, down.

On his fortieth birthday, weeks later, I throw him a surprise party and invite everyone from his department, from his poker games, the bartender from our favorite dive downtown, people from my classes, my teachers, the few friends I have made. He is genuinely surprised, I think, and touched. Everyone dances and drinks until it is nearly dawn. One friend says as he is tumbling out the door, *You guys are such a great couple. You throw the best parties!*

· · ·

The Man I Live With doesn't come to my college graduation. He says he is staying home to get ready for the party, but when I get back to the apartment, nothing has been done. He disappears for longer and longer stretches of time, and occasionally messages appear on our voice mail from numbers I don't recognize. One day I tell him I have been accepted for an internship at a literary magazine in town and the fight we have lasts for days and days. At one point I lock myself in the bathroom and sleep there all night. At another he's cursing at me in every language he knows. He palms my face and pushes me backward onto the couch. I hit my head on the windowsill and see a flash, then darkness. I try to kick him away and he punches me in the hip. I turn into a puddle, dripping from the couch to the floor.

· · ·

In the morning, I say I'm going to my parents' house for a few days, just to visit. I pack a few changes of clothes into a small bag, nothing to raise suspicion. He is playing back-gammon on his computer when I kiss him sweetly on the cheek and walk out the door.

He calls, days later, already very angry, though his voice re-mains calm. At first he tries to bribe me. *Come home and we'll plan a trip to South America.* Then he pleads, and I can feel the decision slipping out from under me. He threatens to tell my parents what a slut I am. He offers to come get me. Finally, I hang up the phone.

When he calls back, Mom answers and calls him a *sonuva-hitch* before slamming down the receiver. He calls back again and Dad tells him that he is bringing me, along with his friend, The State Trooper, to get my things.

He isn't in the apartment when we arrive—me, Dad, and his friend, The State Trooper—or as we stuff the rest of my clothes and books into big black trash bags and toss them in the back of the car. On the way home, Dad pats my leg and asks how I am feeling. I don't hesitate to answer.

Free.

. . .

I get a haircut. I spend whole days writing in coffee shops with My Handsome Friend. I start an internship at the literary magazine, reading submissions from the slush pile, helping to load content into the website. I get a job processing used books at a warehouse. I shop and walk in the street. I run errands and buy groceries. Occasionally, I look over my shoulder and see him walk into or out of a building a half block away. Sometimes I leave through the back exit to avoid him. Other times, I stay right where I am. He approaches me, or doesn't, or leaves a note on my car. *Please come home.* I crumple it up and throw it away. If he follows me, it's always a few cars behind. I sign a lease on an apartment I'll share with My Good Friend.

One night, before we've moved in, My Good Friend drives me back to her place from a bar downtown, and we see a car, his white sedan, following close behind us as we trace the winding unlit road. She drives fast, turning and turning and turning, trying to lose him. We park on the street and run from the car into the house, where we crouch on the living room floor and peer through the blinds with all the lights out. The day I move in to the new apartment he corners me at the hardware store and says he's bought two tickets to Venezuela. He would love to take me there, just to talk. *Just one more trip. Just one last time.* I owe him that much. I want to say, *I don't owe you shit.* But I say nothing. I pretend I haven't heard him. That he's someone I've never met before. I turn my body and go.

. . .

Did you ever, My Newest Therapist finally asks, holding the one list—its intersecting paths—in her hands, *even once, tell anyone the truth about what was happening to you?*

No, not ever, I say. *I still don't understand it myself.*

[seven]

THE DAY BEFORE I am kidnapped and raped by The Man I Used to Live With, My Good Friend talks me into coming with her to a Fourth of July cookout. *A chance to meet new people,* I think. As if relief might flow from unfamiliarity. I have a good time at the cookout, but I catch this strange man watching me each time I toss my hair to the side and take a drag of my cigarette. I find it a little creepy, this staring, but slip him my phone number anyway, and only as I am leaving.

Three weeks later, after I return from My Older Sister's apartment, after I begin seeing The Therapist and The Psychiatrist, and after I begin taking three different kinds of psychotropic medication, The Strange Man calls to say he's having people over for drinks. He knows *what happened* but doesn't say so. He doesn't need to. I need to have a beer, to laugh, and tell jokes with new friends. I need to pretend nothing happened. My family disagrees. My aunt invites us all to her house for a little party—a cousin's birthday— where my aunts and uncles and grandparents hug me as if I am an ancient porcelain doll, as if their embrace might shatter me to pieces. This is the only way anyone will speak to me: the jowly cheek pressed against my cheek, the words clucked right into my ear: *I love you.* The whole thing makes me want to puke. I leave my aunt's party to go home and change: a skirt, a tank top, my favorite pair of flip-flops.

In the apartment of The Strange Man, I sit on the futon in the living room listening to music. When all the other guests leave after hours and hours of drinking, it is either very late or very early, and The Strange Man gets up to make breakfast while I collect beer cans in a big black trash bag. We eat cross-legged on the floor, perched on a pair of pillows. After I've taken three bites of egg and two bites of hash browns, he leans across the plate to kiss me.

It makes me want to puke. Then I am puking.

I come out of the bathroom and find him already apologizing. *It was too soon. I'm sorry. I shouldn't have—not after what you've been through.*

I tell him to shut up. I take him into the bedroom and push him down on the bed. I pull his pants down around his knees. I pull my skirt up around my waist. I don't kiss him and don't let him kiss me. I'm not gentle. This is not lovemaking.

He's still apologizing when I pull down my skirt and walk out the door.

. . .

I return to The Strange Man's apartment night after night, week after week, to play out this same scene. If we're not on the bed, we're on the floor, or the futon, or in the car. Sometimes we're in my apartment, or in a tent at a campsite, or stumbling through the alley after leaving the bar. Sometimes we're at his parents' house, visiting his hometown for a class reunion, or a birthday, or a wedding. It goes on like this until November, four months after the kidnapping, when he asks me to marry him. I'm not at all surprised by the proposal. I've staged the whole thing. I've sent My Good Friend to help pick out the ring. I've told him to take my Dad golfing, to ask for his blessing on the eighth green. I have put these exact words in his mouth: *Will you marry me?*

I agree, not because I love The Strange Man, but because it's what I need.

· · ·

One night, I drag myself home to my apartment after a long day of work. I have found a job as a marketing assistant at the university press, where I look for reviews of the books we have published and cut them out of magazines, or scan them, or type them into a Word document. Tonight, I have had to stay late for some reason or other, and when I leave the office, I stop at the grocery store for a pack of cigarettes and a bag of rice. It is nearly dark outside, and with the blinds closed, it is very dark in the apartment. All the lights are off. I turn my key in the lock, open the door, and walk into the living room, heading for the kitchen, like usual.

It's me, says someone in a wolf mask sitting on my couch. It's a man's voice. A man's body.

I drop all the things in my hands. Everything inside me falls. I don't scream or cry out because in moments I'll be dead. There's a knife in the drawer by the stove. I watch and wait for what comes next.

The man's body stands up, the mask comes off, and underneath it: the face of the man who will become My First Husband. A prank he thinks might be funny. He's not thinking.

It's not funny, I tell him, already pushing him out the door.

·   ·   ·

It's too soon, My Therapist tells me in December, five months after the kidnapping. It's our last session before the holiday break and she's suspicious of my good mood, of the complete and sudden recovery. She asks how I feel now about The Man I Used to Live With, about all that happened. I say *I feel sorry for him. He doesn't need prison; he needs psychiatric help.* One corner of her mouth turns up in a smile. Before I leave I say *See you next week,* though I never return. I tell My Psychiatrist that I feel very happy now and he agrees to take me off the medication. *I've never seen such resilience!* he exclaims, as he begins writing instructions on a pad of paper.

But the truth is, I don't feel happy. I don't feel angry or sorry or frightened or sad. I don't feel anything at all.

It must be the medication, I tell myself. *I'm getting married and I should feel happy.*

All I want is to feel happy.

· · ·

At the wedding, Mom cries and thanks God for sending someone to love me. Dad cries and reaches for her hand.

It is June, eleven months after the kidnapping.

In July, they file for divorce.

Mom is the one who calls, breaking the news like she's telling me the weather. I'm sitting on the futon in the apartment I share with My First Husband, a basket of clean laundry on the coffee table, an ashtray overflowing with cigarette butts. Mom is on the phone saying they've decided that now is as good a time as any. *Everyone is healthy and happy.* I crack a joke, say, *Well it's about time.* I thank her for letting me know and hang up the phone.

I light a cigarette and pick a shirt out of the pile. I'm crying, which doesn't surprise me. It's all I do anymore: cry, smoke, sleep. Today the crying makes me feel like a child: so naive, the hope that my parents might learn to love one another. To forgive. To be happy. To decide, once and for all, to stay together no matter what. All these years I've never understood what actually went so wrong between them. Now I wonder what, if anything, ever went right.

. . .

In August, thirteen months after the kidnapping, I quit my job at the university press and quit the internship at the literary magazine and we move from the college town where there aren't actually any full-time jobs for college graduates, to a city that is not really a city but rather a cluster of small towns. My Older Sister has bought a big house on a tree-lined street; we'll find jobs and live in her basement until we get on our feet. We stack the boxes of our belongings in her garage, and we set up our bed and dresser and bookshelves in the basement room that is probably supposed to be a den. It has a den-like fireplace, den-like wood paneling, and den-like shag carpet on the floor. My First Husband gets a job as a carpenter, and every morning I wake to pack his lunch into a brown paper bag. He asks what I will do today and I say, *Apply for jobs!* but really I will go back to sleep. In the afternoons, My Older Sister leaves for work, and in the evenings, when I am alone in the house with My First Husband, I make dinner: *pescado a la Veracruzana*, the way I learned from watching The Man I Used to Live With. My First Husband and I eat on the couch watching television. Each night, after the first forkful, he grunts and says *Damn, this is delicious,* and then when he is finished he puts his plate or bowl on the edge of the coffee table, as if he plans to take it to the sink later. Each night, he falls asleep on the couch, the dirty dish still at the edge of the coffee table, where he rests his feet, his legs crossed at the ankles.

On the nights when My Older Sister does not work, I make dinner for us. Sometimes we eat at the table like a regular family. Sometimes we go out to bars, where the three of us play pool over cheap beers. If the weather is nice, we grill in the backyard and eat at the picnic table. Sometimes My Younger Sister comes over to the house for dinner, making the short drive from the apartment she shares with other freshmen at her school near the center of the city-that-is-not-a-city, and the three of us stay up late into the night, long after My First Husband has fallen asleep on the couch. We sit outside in the dark, smoking cigarettes and swatting at mosquitoes, making fun of one another and either or both of our parents. We talk and talk and talk. But we never talk about *what happened*. Not about my mountain of credit card debt, or why I start drinking vodka before I've eaten breakfast, or why I can't hold down a job. Not once.

· · ·

We celebrate Christmas at our house. My Older Sister's house. It's the first major holiday since our parents' divorce. Mom arrives the night before, and after we ply her with wine coolers, she says she is eager to start dating. We convince her to put on makeup and fix her hair, and then we take her picture and post it on dating websites. In the morning, My Younger Sister arrives to help cook the giant meal. We are struggling to get everything prepared in time,

My Older Sister whipping the potatoes, a cigarette hanging out of her mouth, My Younger Sister burning her hand putting the rolls in the oven. I am checking the turkey, realizing too late that I have forgotten to remove the giblets. My First Husband's parents arrive, with a laundry basket full of presents to set under the tree. Dad arrives last, in a new sweater the same color as his eyes: spring-sky blue, robin's-egg blue. We've learned only days ago that he's getting married again. Mom has told us how he came to the house and stood on the porch. He knocked on the door and she opened it just a crack, thinking he would ask if he could come back. *I've met someone. We're getting married.* She slammed the door, hard, in his face. Sitting in My Older Sister's house, at opposite ends of the couch, my parents have never looked better. He is tanner, thinner. He drives a new car. Her hair is shorter, higher. Her makeup looks perfect. Her crystal jewelry complements her purple raw silk top. The wine is opened. The food is served. For a few hours, nothing has changed. Our parents go the whole day without speaking.

.   .   .

Two years after the kidnapping, one year after I marry a man I barely know, I am accepted to graduate school and My First Husband and I move from the house we share with My Older Sister to a nearby college town, and we rent an apartment that we have to ourselves. The apartment is on the edge of town, an edge I can reach out and touch: on one side there's a yard, an apartment, a parking lot; on the other side there's a sea of churning, rippling green.

My First Husband has kept his job as a carpenter in the city-that-is-not-a-city and each morning he wakes before sunrise and kisses me on the cheek as he leaves for work. I take my time rising from bed, making breakfast, drinking coffee, choosing my clothes, showering, and pulling my hair into a bun on the top of my head.

I walk into the room and sit in one of the student desks. The students file in, choosing seats, checking their cell phones for messages. The boys wear t-shirts and baggy jeans and the girls wear tank tops and short athletic shorts. One turns to me and whispers, *Have you heard anything about this instructor?* And I say, *Yes, I hear she's a real hard-ass,* before standing and walking to the front of the room. *You can call me Lacy,* I say. *Or if calling me by my first name makes you uncomfortable, "Goddess of the Universe" will also suffice.* I ask my students about images in poems, or the role of gender in the work of lesser-known American novelists. I ask them about rhetorical purpose, and whether an audience's context can change a text. When I ask, they answer. I ask and ask and ask. I have this way of always asking that keeps them looking for answers.

· · ·

I spend each afternoon in the office I share with two women in the basement of the ugliest building on campus, grading my students' papers, checking e-mail, reading stacks and stacks of books for the classes I take. In the evenings, my officemates invite me out to dinner, where we talk the whole time about otherness in British discovery literature, or feminist pedagogical approaches to composition and rhetoric. At these dinners, My First Husband starts trying harder and harder to drink himself into oblivion. I apologize for him. I make excuses: *It's the job,* I say. *It's the commute. He's under so much pressure lately.* On the weekends, he wakes with a hangover and pops a handful of ibuprofen before flopping on the couch to watch NASCAR.

Increasingly, I pick fights with him over nothing. Over his shoes on the coffee table, or the dishes he leaves in the sink. We fight about the clothes he leaves on the floor. We fight about the things he says or does not say while we are fighting. He can't win these arguments. Anything he says, I turn around and use against him. I twist his words until he is apologizing and I am in a rage: slamming furniture against the walls, pulling his clothes from the closet and throwing them out the door. I feel horrified as I'm doing it but I can't stop doing it. I do it for no other reason than because there's no one here to stop me.

· · ·

The Second Therapist's office above the student health center is lit by fluorescent lights. The space is so small that my knees nearly touch the knees of The Second Therapist, who faces me, his back turned to his desk, a pencil and a pad of paper in his hand. After he says hello, shows me the chair I should sit in, he tells me he's a stutterer, though he doesn't actually begin stuttering until I admit why I'm here. I say, *I don't want to have sex with my husband anymore. I'm having these terrible dreams.* His expression does not change. He does not look up from his pad of paper. He asks me to *t-t-t-tell* him about the *d-d-d-d-dreams.* I tell him that two years ago I was kidnapped and raped by a man I knew. *But I don't want to talk about that,* I say. He raises his eyebrows, continues writing. I tell him I want to talk about the panic attacks I've started having anytime I feel My First Husband reaching for me under the sheets. The Second Therapist tells me I should make an *ap-p-p-p-pointment* with a psychiatrist. Her tiny office is right next door to his tiny office. Her office is darker, the overhead lights turned off, the walls stacked higher with books. She asks why I am here. I tell her about the panic attacks, the dreams. I tell her I was kidnapped and raped by a man I used to live with. *I feel so angry. Why am I always so angry?* She looks up from her pad of paper, over her glasses, and asks how much I weigh.

. . .

I remember that the blue pill makes the feeling go away so I start taking it first. The panic goes away, and the anger goes away, and the guilt for the way I've been raging at My First Husband. The white pill makes me sleepy, and dizzy, and costs almost as much money as I earn teaching freshmen to write about literature. The white pill makes it harder to write poems. My body feels very far away. I'm prescribed another pill, and another, and another. And after months of taking these pills, I still don't want to have sex with My First Husband unless I am very very drunk, and even then I close my eyes very tightly and let my thoughts drift somewhere else.

We start couples' counseling and the counselor suggests we go on dates. My First Husband takes me to the movies but I can't decide which one to see. He takes me out to dinner and we sit across from one another at a tiny, candle-lit table. He tries to hold my hand across the white paper tablecloth, but his touch makes my skin crawl. Neither of us can think of a single word to say.

. . .

Meanwhile, I try to have an affair with one of my married colleagues. He starts it, I swear, by looking at me in that hungry, awkward way, saying vaguely inappropriate things that I roll around in my head for hours, trying to understand what he could mean. Increasingly, I stay after class to "study." I sit in his office while he paces, his hands in his pockets, insisting he can't, he can't.

I cross and uncross my legs, begging to differ.

If we meet off campus, it's over coffee—so benign—and in bookstores or libraries. Sometimes he agrees to meet me but then never actually comes. While I wait, in the highest, farthest reaches of the library, I imagine him fucking me, frantic and rough against a stack of musty books. I check them out as souvenirs and bring them back to the apartment, hoping My First Husband finds them.

He doesn't even notice.

He starts humping me in his sleep. I make him sleep in the spare bedroom as punishment. Each night, I hear him whimpering and think of beating him with a rolled-up newspaper.

I can never bring myself to do it.

When he gets drunk at a cookout and pushes me to the ground in front of all of my friends, I kick him out of the apartment. I pack his clothes and CDs into boxes and file for divorce. I cut off all my hair and send him my ponytail through certified mail.

I tell myself I'll never speak to him again.

. . .

Except I do speak to him again. The night I kick him out of our apartment, he shows up on My Older Sister's doorstep.

She calls and asks, *What the fuck?* I haven't told her we're having problems. I haven't told her anything. She can't understand what has gone so wrong between us.

Twice a week he comes to pick me up from our old apartment to take me on another miserable date. I don't let him hold my hand. I don't let him kiss me. I say, *Maybe we should do this only once a week.* Then, *Only twice a month.* Meanwhile, with no one to watch over me, I eat less. I start taking diet pills in addition to the other pills and fall in love with the constant and perpetual neural hum of time travel: how the world slows, how the mind speeds through it.

Back in the apartment I now have to myself, I stay up late reading and writing as long as I want. It's the first time in my life I've actually lived alone. I have only myself to cook for, my own dishes to wash. Only my own laundry to wash and fold. Only one body in the bed: me, mine, my own.

[eight]

I STAND IN the parking lot outside the offices of the literary magazine where I am an intern, unlocking my car, when I hear my name and turn around. I see him crossing the lawn, climbing the hill, walking toward me through the grass. At first I don't recognize him. He wears a twill bucket hat, which is strange because I have never known him to wear hats. He perspires, looks pale. His pupils dart: two pinpricks. Then I think, *Oh. He's high.*

He clears his throat before announcing he no longer wants me back. Actually he's moving far far away. He's going back to Arizona, to be close to his mother. He'll teach in a school. He'll finish his thesis. Maybe he'll write a book.

Relief floods me, and a breath leaves my body, taking with it all reason and care. *But I still have some of your things,* he says neutrally. *Give me a ride to the moving truck—it's just up the block—and then you can follow me home.*

I should know better, should ask him to mail them to me instead. But then he will make excuses. And then we'll argue. And if we argue, he'll pull the words right out from under me. Anything I say, he'll twist around and use against me. He'll twist my words until I'm apologizing and he's in a rage. I should know better, but agree.

. . .

Pulling into the abandoned parking lot, I think *Where is the moving truck?* And just as I suspect but do not believe that something is terribly wrong, I turn to see the stun gun in his outstretched hand. My mind goes blank, empties completely. My stomach enters free fall. He says he will drive now and I can either go peacefully, or in the trunk with permanent nerve damage.

My hand reaches to open the door to run. My legs move so quickly. An opening between the bushes. A backyard. A bike. A ball. He moves more quickly. He catches me by the hair and reels me back in.

You won't escape. He whispers this with his lips near my ear, my hair in his hand, holding the stun gun to my throat, in the place where blood enters my face through the jaw. I hope, but do not pray to God, that he does not pull the trigger.

He pushes me into the passenger seat, sliding me over his lap, puts a black wig and a hat on my head, sunglasses over my face. The lenses are covered in thick black tape. I can see out the sides, but I don't tell him that. When he asks whether I can see, I tell him I can't see. I don't want him to know that I know exactly where we are the whole time he's driving around in circles. That when we pull up to a stoplight near the apartment we once shared, I can see the woman in the next car over. So close I could almost reach out and touch her. She sings to the radio and looks straight ahead, tapping her fingers on the wheel. I could open the door. I could scream or flail or run.

· · ·

He makes a U-turn at the stoplight near the apartment we once shared and goes the opposite direction, fast, through an intersection and down a hill. We exit the boulevard and turn to the right, onto a quiet residential street lined with redbrick apartment buildings I've never seen before. When we pull off the street, into a driveway, behind a tiny four-plex, I can see that half of it is buried underground. I know, having lived here all my life, that burying things during a long summer keeps them cool.

While he comes to my side of the car to open the door I wait in my seat. Terrified. Obedient. He leads me by the arm toward the building, fishes a ring of keys out of his pocket. He opens the storm door first, leans against it while he unlocks the deadbolt, and pushes open the heavy steel door. He leads me across the threshold, into the dark basement apartment, through a dark living room. Out of the edge of the glasses, I see building materials stacked on the floor: scraps of two-by-fours, boxes of nails and screws, a hammer, a drill. Plastic shopping bags discarded in corners. The first door on the right is the one he opens, leads me through, closes behind us and locks. The light comes on. The glasses and wig come off.

. . .

The room, maybe a bedroom under any other circumstances, is small. Thick blue Styrofoam covers every surface but the gray-carpeted floor: the walls, the ceiling, the door. I can see no windows, but I'm not looking for them yet. All I see is the moment of my death, not far away.

In the middle of the room there's a giant wooden chair constructed of two-by-fours and four-by-fours. Like an electric chair. A hole in the seat opens to a bucket under-neath. Two steel U-bolts are attached to the thick wooden arms with galvanized fencing staples. A choke collar hangs from the headrest.

. . .

I'm going to rape you now, he says while I undress. *Or I'm sure that's what you'll call it, anyway.* In the corner of the room there are several sheets of paper folded into a neat square: a letter he'll read to me after he's bolted me into the chair, after he's fed me a turkey sandwich, his hands hot and sticky with his own semen. While I'm swallowing and choking and spitting it out he explains that I'll call My Good Friend to tell her I've decided to take him back. On the phone, I clear my throat nervously and tell her I'll come by in a few days to pick up my clothes. She wants to know what clothes. *Sorry, I can't come by tonight,* I say. *I'll come by in a few days.* She's so confused. *Where are you? What is happening?* I can't speak, with him sitting right beside me, demanding I hang up the phone. I want to say, *Send help.* Instead I say, *I don't know.*

. . .

Or maybe the phone call happens first. At one point he tells me to put his penis in my mouth—he's so angry he can't get it hard for this—and at another he tightens the dog collar around my neck, gesturing toward the places he's planted explosives in the walls, a camera in the corner, a detonator in the kitchen. All the possible outcomes play like a movie in my head: He cues the explosion. Pieces of my body fly in every direction. But then he puts his face close to mine and says *No one can hear you. Go ahead and scream.*

. . .

I do not scream.

I sit on the edge of the mattress, which is sloppily dressed with a fitted white sheet covered by a clear plastic sheet, covered by a goose-down duvet, the same one he gave me on my birthday. The mattress lies on the floor in the corner.

He doesn't live here. No one lives here.

He asks who might be expecting me. I consider whom to call, who could best handle answering the last phone call I ever make. Not my parents. They aren't expecting me. I have just moved into my new apartment, and I planned to spend the night unpacking. Yesterday, my parents took me to the store to get new sheets, new towels, a new comforter for the bed. The mattress hasn't been delivered yet. Mom said, *I don't think we can afford to keep setting you up all over again like this.*

I lie and call My Good Friend. She'll tell me later that she knew something was wrong. She spends the whole night driving around looking for me: the old apartment I used to share with him, the new apartment, my favorite bars downtown, ditches beside the road.

He says, *I'm going to rape you now.* And it doesn't matter that I am on my period, because he pulls my tampon out by the string and lays it beside the mattress. The police will find it later and catalogue it into evidence. My blood pools on the clear plastic sheet, which they will also catalogue into evidence.

. . .

At first, I have a body, a wild animal body I throw and thrash against his cage. I almost break a limb before he catches me in his hands. I growl and hiss and bare my teeth. But then, my body is not a wild animal body. It's a human girl body: the two arms pinned, a cross; the two legs spread, a tomb. It's the mind that goes thrashing so wildly. The body remains calm. The body undresses and lays itself down.

But the mind goes thrashing so wildly. The body lays itself down on a clear plastic sheet, hears but does not listen to the soup of human-like speech boiling in its ears, spilling exactly the length and width of the room. The mind skitters safely out of reach.

The body lays itself down but does not know with precision in which direction or at what point, if any, in the future it will rise and go. Or if it will be physically possible, the future having maybe splintered the body into a thousand wet-shining shards.

Underneath, bedrock unbuckles with the thrust of vast tectonic plates, skidding at this very moment over an ocean of white-hot magma in the body's every orifice.

But the mind goes thrashing. The mind goes thrashing away from the body, which does not move a muscle, does not move an inch from the spot in which it is unraveling, will be unraveling, has been unraveling since.

[nine]

THREE YEARS AFTER the kidnapping I can't find anyone to sleep with me. My married colleague won't sleep with me. My single colleagues won't sleep with me. My professors at graduate school are too gay or too old to sleep with me. Tonight, I have just come home from a night of dancing with my girlfriends—the first without my wedding ring. I am drinking vodka from a plastic cup and blowing my cigarette smoke out the window, browsing around the Internet—*not exactly a dating site,* My Good Friend tells me in the e-mail—when I see the photo of a man who might sleep with me. I e-mail him first, a hokey pickup line. He writes back almost instantly. We e-mail many times a day, every day, for weeks. We tell flirty jokes, trading the grand narratives of our lives, the minutiae of our hobbies, and then he asks me for an actual in-person date.

I tell my officemates I'm supposed to meet him at his apartment and they think I am insane. *You're not even divorced yet,* they scold. One insists that I call her five minutes before I arrive, and she will call after I've been there ten minutes to make sure he hasn't hacked me into pieces.

He greets me with a giant smile—he's blushing a little—and a kiss on the cheek. Inside, he offers me something to drink. We spend most of the evening on his couch, smoking cigarettes, sipping from tall glasses of flat water. We take turns talking: his voice, like water, puts me at ease. He tells me what he knows about loss.

I spill all my beans.

Instead of the predictable response—the shock, the hand over the mouth or to the chest, *I'm so sorry*—The Man Who Might Sleep with Me says something like *Shut UP! That did NOT happen to you!!!*

I laugh. It is a good first date.

He reaches over to hold my hand halfway through the high-budget kung fu movie. My palm sweats and I hope he doesn't notice. Maybe he thinks his palm is sweating.

Before the credits roll, we're making out on the couch like a couple of teenagers. I try to unbutton his pants. He takes my hands in his and brings them to his lips. I try again, pulling him close, closer. Closer.

But this man doesn't unbutton his pants, or pull my shirt over my head. He kisses me on the forehead and offers to make me a cup of tea.

It's not what I'm expecting, not even what I want, but I agree.

. . .

At first I say I don't want a boyfriend. I'm not interested in a relationship. All I want is someone to fuck me senseless, to pound me until I'm raw and shaking. I want to be held down, pushed aside, flipped over, and smacked. I want to be choked, chained, tied to the floor. I want to bruise, to bleed, to cry out *please stop please don't stop.* I want him to leave after it's done. And then I'll stand up, take a shower, turn on the television.

. . .

But what I get is two hands on my shoulders when I'm screaming in my sleep. I get a hand on my back, in my hair. I get kisses on my cheek. I get glazed salmon and a glass of chardonnay. I get mixed CDs, and antique books, a shiny new cigarette case. I get picked up after work. I get dinner and a movie. I get a drawer, one side of the closet, a trash can in the bathroom. I get the best spot on the couch, a whole wall for my bookshelves, one half of the rent and the bills.

. . .

I am packing my books into boxes, preparing to move in with this boyfriend, when Dad and his new wife come to town and take me out to lunch. We scooch into a booth in a corner near the window. We are on the second floor of a café in the artsy downtown district: Dad and His New Wife across from me, their backs to the restaurant, my back, like always, to the wall, where no one can approach me from behind. At first, things are tense. I haven't spent much time with His New Wife yet, and it's clear she's still sizing me up. She wants to like me, wants to be liked in return. She has brought me a gift: a pair of silver earrings. I haven't brought anything for her. I carry only my wallet, my cell phone, the shiny new cigarette case.

Dad asks how school is going, whether I have decided to go on for the PhD. I talk about a class I've been teaching at a local shelter, a poetry workshop for women recovering from substance abuse: their stories, their lives—always in limbo, always tentative. I'm writing a paper, I say, presenting at a conference this fall, two more in the spring. I ask His New Wife to tell me how they met. A blind date he didn't know he was on, she jokes. A mutual friend set it up. He has already told me this story: how after the divorce he would leave each day before dawn to work at the power plant, sleeping each night in a spare bedroom above his friend's garage. The mutual friend invited them both over for dinner, where Dad was polite to this woman, but tired. He left early to go to bed. His New Wife laughs at this now, as she stirs sweetener into her tea. On their first actual date, they went to dinner. Before the waiter brought their drinks Dad learned they share the same birthday. By the time the bread came, he learned she loves to laugh. Sometime between the salad and the soup, he came alive again, he says.

She was across from him, looking so beautiful, sipping her wine. She was talking about her children, saying, *I have an infinite capacity to love. And that was it,* my father says, *I knew she was the one.* I smile. I'm happy for him, really. I'm about to say so when the waiter comes to take our order.

.   .   .

From the windows in the apartment I share with My Boyfriend I can see a brick wall, so close I could almost reach out and touch it. Between our windows and the brick wall, there is a shaft of light, a small alleyway that leads out to the street. There is only one window in our apartment that looks out toward that light, in a little alcove where we've put an armchair, a lamp, and an ashtray. On the days when I do not take classes or teach, this is where I work, my annotated copy of a postmodern Irish novel, or a stack of student papers, or poems from workshop spread out on my lap. My Boyfriend walks to work in the morning, and at noon he comes home for lunch, though we only lie down in bed together and nap. At night, I write poems while he paints, or replants his aquarium, or designs at his desk. If he reads one of my poems, he says things like, *The image at the end reminds me of what Blavatsky says about the finite's relationship to the infinite.* And then he goes to pull a book off the shelf and shows me an illustration and then we are having a conversation about that.

At night, I stay up long after he has fallen asleep beside me in the bed, his arm draped over my waist, listening to the voices coming through our window from the alleyway, the men and women, all drunk, stumbling out of the bar downstairs. Now a woman yells, *You're an asshole, a fucking asshole!* Her voice growing hoarse with the force of every syllable. I remember that hoarseness, how it scratches from my throat into my chest, into my fingers and toes. I remember how The Man I Used to Live With stands above me, his red face contorted, the veins full to bursting in his forehead. He's squeezing my face in his hand. Now the woman cries softly in the alleyway. The man calls her baby. *Baby,* he says. *C'mon, baby.* From this bed, where I am almost sleeping, it makes a kind of sense: this is why I could not love him the way he wanted to be loved.

. . .

My sisters and I spend the holiday together, like usual: all of us on Christmas Eve at Mom's house, all of us on Christmas Day at Dad's. Mom's house—the house she shared with my father, the house she got in the divorce—feels dark and empty this year, even with all of us here: all of the doorways closed or covered with blankets, the heat vents in my old bedroom closed, the floral-print couch pulled into the dining room off the kitchen. My sisters and I exchange questioning looks. *It doesn't usually look this way,* I whisper to

My Boyfriend as we sit down. *I'm happy,* Mom tells us over dinner—a pot each of chowder and chili—*happier than I've ever been.* She's sewing more than ever. She's taken a part-time job. She's dating someone from church. My Boyfriend asks to see something she's working on and she shoots him down with a look. *Don't expect me to get attached to you,* she tells him, as my sisters and I file off to bed. *I've learned nothing is permanent.*

. . .

Dad greets us at the door in a new sweater: pine-tree green. Fern-shoot green. A smile stretching from ear to ear. His New Wife emerges from the kitchen to hug us all, even My Boyfriend, though this is the first time they've met. In the Victorian house they've bought together, glass beads hang on strings from every window, casting prisms around the rooms. Dad insists we sit on the new gray corduroy couch: me, each of my two sisters, My Boyfriend. His New Wife pours glasses of wine. My grandmother arrives and we all sit down to dinner: spaghetti and meatballs, a loaf of crusty French bread, a salad of spring greens. *This is not what I would consider holiday food,* my grandmother says, in her way. She turns to My Boyfriend. *Now tell me: What kind of man are you?*

. . .

Four years after the kidnapping I learn I've been accepted into a prestigious writing program in Texas for a PhD. My Boyfriend and I trade in both of our crappy cars for one that can pull all of our belongings in a U-Haul trailer. My Boyfriend finds work quickly in our new city. He drives the new car to work each day while I catch a ride to campus. In the evenings, my classmates invite us out to dinner, where we talk about semiotics or the ubiquity of ampersands in workshop lately, or the landscape as form in avant-garde poetics. At these dinners, My Boyfriend talks to the spouses or boyfriends or girlfriends of my classmates about more interesting things. They plan to make a band together called The Significant Others. *None of us know how to play instruments. YET!* As a present for his birthday, I arrange a behind-the-scenes tour at the downtown aquarium, where a short executive with shaved hands leads us through the rooms and rooms of filtration systems and lets us peer into the tops of giant glass tanks. In the pump room for a 150,000-gallon aquarium in the restaurant, the short executive with shaved hands introduces us to a scuba diver, who is preparing to jump in. *It happens sometimes,* the short executive says. *Let's say a couple is dining at the restaurant. He wants to propose. For a nominal fee, the scuba diver will jump in and hold up a sign: WILL YOU MARRY ME?* The scuba diver nods, shows us the sign. The executive asks if we want to go down to the restaurant and see. I think, *Is it us? Is he proposing to me?* My Boyfriend holds open the door of the pump room, follows me down the stairs. The short executive with shaved hands leads us down into the dining room, where a man is already kneeling in front of a table. The woman is crying, nodding. People in the restaurant are clapping. My Boyfriend claps; he's watching the man stand up. He looks at me. He takes my hand.

He asks for nothing in return.

. . .

Five years after the kidnapping, a friend from my writing program throws me a birthday party at her house. I buy a dress to celebrate all the things that are suddenly going so well. There is music and food and it seems like hundreds of people. All of my new friends are there, and My Boyfriend's friends from work. At midnight, my friend brings a cake out with twenty-seven lit candles and everyone sings, just to me. It makes me so happy I could nearly explode. They ask me to toast. I say something a little silly, a little drunk, about how I am feeling so very grateful.

As everyone raises their glasses, My Boyfriend interrupts, insisting he also has something to say. He says, *I love you. I want to spend my life with you,* and pulls a velvet box from his pocket. I am completely surprised, completely not expecting it, struck completely mute. I am crying, covering my mouth with my hand. I take him in my arms and say *Yes yes yes.*

. . .

In the photos of our wedding, we both look radiant and happy. We gather at the park with our family and the friends we have made in this city. My parents stand beside me, Dad with His New Wife, Mom with the man she has married only weeks ago. Beside My Husband stand his father and sister and godparents and aunts. The vows we exchange are simple.

I promise to treat you as my equal in all things.

[ten]

IN A VARIATION of Schrödinger's famous thought experiment, we are instructed to imagine the steel chamber from the perspective of the cat. Except the cat has been replaced by a person, and the poison gas and radioactive trigger have been replaced with another life-terminating device— an assault rifle, let's say. Every ten seconds, the weapon is either deployed, killing the person, or it makes an audible *click* and the person survives. Outside the chamber, those two outcomes—death and survival, the bullet wound and the sound of the empty chamber—exist in equal probability, creating a paradox as in the original experiment. Inside the chamber, the person might have been killed or not killed—*click*—but because the mind is bound to follow whatever path does not lead to death, and because it isn't possible to experience having been killed, the person's only possible experience is of having survived the experiment, regardless of the odds.

. . .

Every few months, or years, or days, or some random and indeterminate amount of time, I enter his name into a search engine. I look for any news: an address, a phone number, a blog post, any indication of whether he is in this country or out of it, whether he is trying to find me or is content to let me go. At first I collected the information in a real, tangible manila file I kept in a drawer of my desk. Now it's in a folder of bookmarks on my computer.

I can open the folder and see that the first story about the kidnapping runs in the local city paper on July 7, 2000: two days after I escape. In the upper-left corner, there is a tiny, low-resolution photo of the accused. Unattractive, unassuming, he does not, even now, look to me like a rapist. But there, above the photo, the headline reads: GRAD STUDENT SOUGHT IN RAPE. The article, written by a female journalist on the local city paper's staff, gets the facts only slightly wrong. She writes that the victim *found her car outside covered by a tarp with the keys still inside.* The keys were not in the car, but on a table in the apartment. I remember this because I spotted the key chain, a lizard, which My Good Friend had made for me a few nights earlier, stringing green and white plastic beads onto a length of clear plastic twine.

. . .

For years I imagine the female journalist as elderly, as a sort of female journalist archetype, so hardened by the decades spent covering petty or disturbing small-town crimes that she can't be bothered to get the facts exactly right. But when I enter her name into a search engine, I discover that she is not an elderly journalist, but a woman roughly my age, who had only recently graduated when she wrote the article. For some reason, this allows me to forgive her for the factual inaccuracies. I bookmark her website and add it to the folder on my computer.

.   .   .

An article appearing in the Tuesday, July 11, 2000, issue of the same local city paper warns readers that the *search for the man accused of abducting and sexually assaulting his former girlfriend has become an international pursuit.* The article describes how, after tracking his credit card activity, detectives learned that The Suspect purchased an airline ticket to Mexico, and then another one to Venezuela, where he stayed for a time at a resort on the coast. *He's a very intelligent individual who's scaring me,* says a captain on the local police force. A professor from the Spanish department describes The Suspect as *erratic and disorganized* as a scholar, but *affable, . . . a gifted, erratic dilettante.* The professor asks not to be named. I read the article from the safety of the home I share with My Husband and our children, wondering why this professor could have possibly thought he, of all people, was at risk.

. . .

Subsequent articles describe slim chances of extradition: under a provision of the recently revised Venezuelan constitution The Suspect's dual citizenship with Venezuela and the United States protects him from extradition. *It's not clear*, the captain says, *when or whether The Suspect can be returned.* The authority of the United States government to extradite in this case depends on interpretations of citizenship based on the laws of Venezuela, matters that can easily end up in foreign courts. *It's a very difficult and complicated area of law.*

One article in the university student paper describes the process of sending the warrants to Venezuela: Interpol notifies the Venezuelan government that one of its citizens is wanted on felony charges in the United States, but officials there may or may not arrest him and transport him to the US embassy. Even though a treaty has existed between the United States and Venezuela since 1922, the article explains, the new constitution under Chávez makes things a little more complicated.

. . .

The article in the university student paper is written by a woman I will meet one night, after I have returned to my new apartment, after I have started taking medication, and have found a job at the university press, and have started fucking the man who will become My First Husband. My Good Friend and I have gone out drinking. We're settling into a booth when she points to a woman across the bar. The friend of a friend of a friend. The woman sees us both, comes over to our table, sits down. Maybe she introduces herself as a journalist before putting her hand on my hand. *I've been writing about what happened to you,* she says in a near whisper, her tongue piercing clicking against the back of her teeth. *Don't worry—click—your story's safe with me.*

. . .

According to a resume he has posted on a website for free-lance translators, in the years between 2000 and 2007 he works a variety of editing, translating, and interpreting jobs, sometimes for large, international corporations. He spends time as an interpreter for the Venezuelan lower courts. He translates a Motorola cell phone instruction manual and its product description from English into Spanish. He edits several titles on conflict management for the University for Peace.

During those same years I marry. I divorce. I marry again. I change addresses at least once every year. I give birth to a child. Less and less frequently I e-mail The Detective to ask about the case. *Any changes? Any news?*

. . .

One Halloween, seven years after the kidnapping, an e-mail from him appears in my inbox. He has just been released from jail in Venezuela after a failed extradition attempt and wants me to finally and officially drop the charges in the United States. *I hope you'll consider my plea,* he writes. *And I would like to hear back from you even if it's just to say that you're sorry. Even if you decide not to respond to this message, I wish you all the best.*

I close my laptop screen and draw the blinds. I lock all the doors and turn off the television. I pull my daughter out of bed and call her father in a cold sweat. We're hiding on the floor in the kitchen when he finally bursts through the front door, dressed as Clark Kent for a Halloween office party, his tie loosened and pulled to the side, his shirt half unbuttoned, the blue fabric of his Superman t-shirt visible underneath. I call The Detective, who now works as a lead investigator for the county's prosecuting attorney. He wants me to respond to the e-mail, to try to bait him, to lure him back to the United States one last time.

. . .

That night we trick-or-treat like regular people. In the photo, I'm dressed as a sheriff, looking like I've seen a ghost. Or I am a sheriff-ghost. We walk up and down the streets of our suburban neighborhood. My daughter keeps pulling her hand from my hand. I am holding her too tight, picking her up too often, trying too hard to rush her back home. All the while I'm looking and looking and looking over my shoulder.

In the morning I write to The Detective to tell him I can't do it. I can't set the trap. I can't be the bait. *I have too much to lose.* I remove my profile from all the social networking sites. I call all of my former employers and ask them to pull my bio down from their websites. It's the only thing I can think to do.

. . .

But somehow he's the one who disappears. Maybe he's been murdered or has changed his name. I can see that his ex-wife and half brothers are "friends" on Facebook, a fact that makes me both worry and hope. Maybe one of them knows where he is, whether he is still living, but I can't bring myself to write to them.

Each morning I look in the backseat of the car before I pull out of my driveway. I search the rearview mirror while driving my children to school. I scan the parking lot before unbuckling them from their seats.

Back home, I sit at my desk and watch for him out my window. I do not leave the house after dark. I turn the lights off at bedtime and lie awake in fear that he will come into my house and kill me while I am sleeping.

If I sleep, he brings a gun into my dreams.

. . .

I used to have this wooden comb he bought for me on a beach in Mexico. A few yards up the beach, lobsters smoked over half-drum grills. The old woman came to our blanket, putting beautiful carved things in my hands: a horse, a bracelet, the comb. After I'd used it on my hair every night for years and years, the handle snapped off. And then I kept it in a drawer until I caught my daughter running it through her hair and finally threw it away.

I still have coins from Belgium and Hungary and Spain. I think I have a few Danish kroner tucked into a book somewhere. I kept the watercolor paintings we bought from a street artist in Prague—they hang in the only hallway of my house—and a stein I stole from a *Biergarten* in Germany. I never wear the beautiful silk shawl from Spain, though I've kept it. I kept no fewer than thirty postcards I never wrote on or sent.

I left behind the two skirts he bought for me in a market in Amsterdam. But I kept a strand of glass beads he bought from the same market, the same day, each orb an imperfect apology for the bruise on my face. *An accident,* he insisted. Or maybe he admitted he did not love me. Afterward, we slid into a series of low-slung booths to order hash from a menu and sink into a wordless haze, which sent us toward the narrow red-lit streets, toward those women who stand and kneel and bend to press against the glass. I envied them that glass, the explicit transaction, the lock on the door. What was the word there for silence? Something about an attic room. A flowering tree: how the blossoms open and are lost instantly.

.   .   .

In the transcript of the Venezuelan extradition trial, he testifies that he was arrested only by chance, for having mistakenly associated with a member of a drug cartel, that only after questioning him about his associate—whom he barely knows—did the police conduct a background search on him and find the charges: kidnapping, rape, forcible sodomy, felonious restraint. After he admits that the Interpol case exists, he explains to the court that they must understand that this is a ridiculous farce initiated by a bunch of hillbillies. He explains how it looks in the United States for an older man to be with a beautiful young girl, *and to be Latin on top of that, in a place where to be Latin is to be black.*

After he explains that he lived with this young girl for years until she abruptly cut him off, he admits he did follow her, he did take over the use of her car, he did bring her against her will to an apartment where he asked her to apologize. *I was affected. I wanted explanations.* He tells the court that, after the girl finally did apologize, *We cried together and had consensual relations, as couples do.*

He had to leave to run some errands, he tells the court, and admits tying the girl's hands to the chair. When he returned, twenty minutes later, the police were already there. At that point he fled and decided to return to his own country, where he's been living ever since, working at his job, paying his taxes like a good citizen.

The only time he's talked to the girl since returning to Venezuela, he says, is when she called to beg his forgiveness. He says the girl told him at the time that she wanted to withdraw the charges but was afraid to because the authorities would punish her for giving false testimony.

The gringos, he says, *solicited an extradition for an American. But I'm Venezuelan.* The court records from the trial say this is exactly why they release him and deny the extradition. The Venezuelan government, the court rules, has the responsibility to protect its citizens.

. . .

I know the case will never come to trial. The FBI and Interpol will never catch him outside Venezuela's borders. And the Venezuelan government will never hand one of its citizens over to another nation's authorities.

And for that I am grateful.

It spares me a certain set of uncomfortable choices: whether or not to travel to the trial with my children, how much and when to explain, whether or not to meet his gaze across the courtroom, or to confront him in the hallway, or in his cell in the courthouse, or in the shuffle before they drag him ceremoniously away. Where would I begin? Thirteen years after the kidnapping, the possibility of sitting in the same room with him seems so perilous: a precipice beyond which I can't see. I'm spared the shame of the witness stand, of having to say out loud what exactly happened in the back bedroom of the basement apartment. Could I speak those words? I'm spared the sentence he might serve, which would begin and end. And then he would walk free.

. . .

I haven't seen the official case file at the offices of the county prosecuting attorney. Because the case is still active and open, The Lead Investigator says he can't copy and send me the file, but he'll let me see it anytime I want. He doesn't see any reason I couldn't visit the evidence room, where they've stored the snakeskin-print shirt I was wearing the day of the kidnapping, and my favorite jeans—the ones with a hole in the right knee, and the bracelet with the carnelian stone Mom bought off QVC for my twenty-first birthday, and the plastic sheet he used to cover the mattress on the floor, and the down duvet he brought home from Denmark, and his handwritten notes, and the used tampon he pulled from my body, and the tissue smeared with my blood that police found on the floor. They still have the rifle.

I can go see it anytime I want, The Lead Investigator says.

But I won't go, not ever. Because I already know what it looks like, how it smells. I already know the sound each time the trigger is pulled.

Click.

Click.

Click.

[eleven]

THE DREAM GOES like this: I am in a mall, or the post office, or the supermarket, or the bank with my two children. People mill around us, each face like every other face. I am running late, or I am too early to meet a friend for lunch, or I am trying to retrieve the cell phone ringing in my diaper bag. I see him approaching at first only out of the corner of my eye—intent, purposeful, his jaw set crookedly, his snarling upper lip—and my stomach transforms from a regular stomach into a black hole stomach that begins to swallow me, and all of dream-time, which moves more slowly any way. In some dreams I cry out in a wet, drawn-out way—a baby deer bleeding to death in my throat. In other dreams I beg for help from the nearest stranger. I try to ask the bank teller to call the police but my mouth is full of feathers. Sometimes I call the police myself. They never come in time. I ask a kind-looking woman to pretend my children are her own. *Keep them safe,* I croak. The kind-looking woman, my daughter, my infant son—he will kill them all and make me watch. In the end, he smirks a little, and even the dream-time stops.

. . .

On my very worst days I can't handle my children touching me. I can't handle seeing them or hearing their voices asking me for things. They're always asking for things. My daughter asks for a glass of milk, and when I pour it for her, hand her the cup, she slams her hands down on the counter and demands juice. It's not really about the milk or the juice. My son climbs on the dining table, or clings, screaming, to my legs while I'm making dinner. It's not food or milk or a nap he wants.

I don't know how to give him what he wants.

I don't want to give him what he wants.

As I slap the tiny hand pulling up the hem of my skirt— *No!*—I can't stop myself. I'm already fleeing from this moment to another, closing all the doors behind me as I go.

. . .

At dinner, weeks after our honeymoon in Belize, we tell our friends about the results of the pregnancy test, and everyone sits without speaking, mouths hanging open, before one friend begins clapping very slowly, as if this were the climactic scene in an Afterschool Special. Our friends say *Oh, that's wonderful, just wonderful.* But then soon they are no longer calling us for karaoke night or to come over for dinners in the backyard or to meet them at the bar after teaching or for breakfast at the coffee shop.

I stop smoking the day I learn I am pregnant, and I stop drinking and taking my medication. At first the hardest part is withdrawal: some parts of my brain waking, misfiring, shooting sparks in every direction; other parts drifting slowly off to sleep. I can't remember my students' names anymore and begin calling them all "Bob." *Can anyone share thoughts about how Offred subverts patriarchal control . . . Bob? Bob?* I can't write poems anymore, not without a drink, not without staying up until two in the morning, not without a lit cigarette in my hand. Then the hardest part is the puking. How, once again, six years after the kidnapping, I am always puking.

One afternoon I can't get out of bed. My Husband rubs my back while I sob hysterically. He asks, *What's wrong? What's wrong?* The truth is: I can't stand waiting for it anymore. *I wish the other shoe would drop already,* I say. He does not call me hormonal because he knows better. Instead he asks, *What if this is the other shoe?*

. . .

When summer comes, My Husband and I buy a video camera and drive all morning and afternoon and evening, from Texas to the town with only three stoplights, thinking we'll stay for a long visit. We'll film a documentary or research my genealogy or practice time-lapse photography. We spend hours and hours and hours filming interviews with my grandparents and parents and aunts and uncles, and in the process I learn that my mother grew up very very poor, and that my father grew up working very very hard, and suddenly their life together makes a kind of sense. My father tells me that when his own father died of metastatic melanoma six weeks after I was born, he lost his best friend in the world. It's a grief that brings him to tears, twenty-eight years later. My mother tells me about her breast cancer, and how she woke up from surgery and went into convulsions when she felt the pain, and again when the doctor removed the bandages. She tells me how she was lucky to survive. *It was the aggressive kind. It wouldn't have taken any time* and then she is crying very hard, and squeezing my hand very tightly, and asking me to forgive her. *I'm so sorry, Lacy.* She is looking intently into my eyes, mascara running from behind her glasses, and saying that if there is one thing I absolutely must teach my child it is how to love. *I will do better,* she says, squeezing my hand. *I swear I am trying to be better.*

. . .

Sometimes I dream we are having a civilized conversation. I am writing at my favorite coffee shop, or at an outdoor café, or I am turning the pages of a magazine under an umbrella on the beach. I hear a voice say, *I thought that was you,* and he sits down. In this dream he talks and talks, waving a hand in his usual way. He's moved on, he says. He's moved far far away. It's such a reassuring thing to hear. I almost forget to feel afraid.

. . .

It's two in the morning and I'm shaking. My Husband is the only person in the hospital room and I have no words. I'm trying to communicate to him that I want to escape. I want him to help me crawl out of my skin. *Help me. Up. Out. Help. Out.*

The anesthesiologist is on his way. He's taking his sweet time. Maybe he is listening to headphones and nodding to the nurses in the hall. *How you doin'.* I want to tear my face off. I want to use My Husband as a footstool, to climb him and hang from the ceiling, which seems like a safer place to ride this out than in the bed.

Suddenly: a rupture. A little relief from the pressure. But just when I start panting and clawing and growling, the anesthesiologist comes sauntering in. He barks at me: *Sit up. Lean over. Hold still.* One gloved hand holds my shoulder—latex smell, condom smell—the other pushes a needle into my back.

. . .

The body goes thrashing. The father of my child, gray-faced and sweating, a deer caught in headlights. He smiles a polite smile. The body breathes and bears down. Breathes and bears down. The body opens its mouth and a sound flies out. One of the nurses pushes the code-blue button on the wall—*click*—and while I am screaming and bearing down hard enough to leave myself with two black eyes, every nurse and doctor on the floor rushes the room. A nurse mounts the bed, climbs on top of me, and pushes downward on my belly with the heels of both hands until our daughter tears through me. One doctor cuts the cord without a word, and another carries her body away.

The mind listens for the cough, the wail, the first undrowning breath. But there is only silence. Only the stretch of time. Not even all these arms can hold it in.

I open my eyes. My Husband stands motionless, staring out the door. People I've never seen before tell me I've done a great job.

Where is my baby?

. . .

The doctor explains in a calm voice that the baby is fine. He says the words *shoulder dystocia* and *intensive care.* I don't understand him. *Where is my baby?* I'm trying to climb out of the bed to find the baby I am certain is dead. The nurses hold me down, tell me to stay put. *Where is my baby?* The doctor says they are checking her to make sure everything is fine. *She is fine.* I don't believe him. *Is she dead? Did she die? The baby is fine,* he says. He is smiling and washing his hands. A nurse wipes between my legs, still in the stirrups, with a rough towel, swabs me with iodine, begins stitching me back together. *Where is my baby?* I am shaking—the pain and terror passing through me in waves. My Husband smoothes back my hair, runs his thumbs across my cheeks, wet with sweat and tears. He smiles a reassuring smile. The doctor says everything is fine.

I am allowed a drink of water. I close my eyes and rest my head on the pillow. While the nurse stitches the wound that is gaping and open, I am trying to stitch the mind back into the body. The door opens, and a nurse enters, carrying something in her arms. She places it beside me in the bed: the baby, bruised and breathing.

In the story I have told myself about how this would go, about how the baby will make everything better, I know this child instantly; I see her face and the past falls away. Life starts over at this moment, with this child I have always known.

But now that I am looking into her face, I don't feel anything at all.

.   .   .

It's morning, seven years after the kidnapping, and I'm closing the door to her room for the third time today, afraid to let it catch. *Sleep while the baby sleeps,* that's what everyone tells me. As if I've never heard that before. As if it's that simple. My daughter has never been a good sleeper, and today she's at her worst. I need sleep more than I need to finish grading my students' writing assignments, more than I need to finish my dissertation, or eat breakfast, or shower, or get dressed. But if I move from where I am standing with this doorknob in my hand she might wake up and hours might pass before she sleeps again. Maybe I could sleep standing this way: frozen for a long, long time.

I let go of the knob—*click*—she coughs, stirs, howls. White-hot sparks shoot through each exhausted limb, my hands contract into fists. Maybe I could leave her here. Take the keys and trudge through the snow to sleep in the car at the end of the driveway, far from the reach of sound or care. I don't care. I could climb to the roof's edge and fall head-first. No child has ever died of crying. The ladder hangs from the far wall of the garage.

I lift her shrieking body from the crib and lay her down on the terry-cloth changing pad. I watch myself from the safe distance: wrestling the naked child out of and back into her clothes, brushing a slice of greasy hair out of my face, the pajamas hanging dankly from my shoulders and hips. I observe her. I observe myself. I prop her body against my chest, her head lolling forward against my neck. Her breath like milk. She bawls into that nook as we shuffle toward the window.

Outside, snow blankets the full reach of each tree's branches, the minivan in my neighbors' driveway, the shut mouth of their black iron mailbox, our gutterless street. A single brown bird shoots from the hedge. With my free hand, I open the window. The cold air blows in. Her cries multiply; I shut out the sound. Her face purples, ajar. I feel nothing as her velvet crown slides into the crook of my elbow, rooting for me. Always rooting. She bites once, hard, as we lean into the rocking chair's curve, wedged between this moment and another.

.   .   .

Dad tells only one story about me, his middle child, a toddler, found pecking the buttons on the television console with a fat, sticky finger. He scolds me, tells me to stop. I ignore him, keep pushing the buttons, switching the channel each time. He raises his voice, and I ignore that, too. He smacks my outstretched hand. *Hard,* he says. *But you don't cry or wince or turn away. You set your jaw, raise your hand, keep pushing that button.*

Mom reminds me how, when I was a teenager and arguing with her every day, she started putting this hex on me: *When you grow up and have children I hope one of them is exactly like you.*

I think now that maybe that hex came through: If I tell my daughter to stop jumping on the bed, she climbs onto the dresser. If I ask her to behave while I take an important call, she throws a tantrum before drawing a beard on her face with a red permanent marker. If I tell her to pick up her toys in the kitchen, she empties a box of cereal on the floor. I might put her in time out, or yell until I'm blue in the face. She does not cry or wince or turn away.

It makes me furious. I want her to behave, even just a little. But she fights me about which shoes to wear, which bowl to use for cereal. She fights me about which clothes she'll wear and ruin. She fights me about the punishment she gets for fighting me. She can't win these arguments, because no matter how big and loud and strong she gets, I can always get bigger, louder, stronger. I want her to be a little afraid of me. *It's the only way to break her,* I think. *This defiant, fearless child.* And it's all I want right now: to break her. Just a little.

. . .

But then we are driving to the house where my daughter attends preschool; she is thrashing in her car seat, screaming at the top of her lungs. The body takes a breath, turns up the radio. My daughter spits milk in a wide stream on the upholstery of my first-ever brand-new car and pushes Goldfish crackers irretrievably into the horizontal crevice between the back passenger window and the door. The body takes a breath, adjusts the rearview mirror. But when my daughter starts kicking the back of my elbow with the pointy toe of her pink cowboy boot, I snap, and lean into the backseat of the car and smack her knee. *Hard.* Hard enough that she grows silent and stares out the window with giant tears rolling down her cheeks. I drag her and her tiny little backpack into the preschool house. The teacher greets us at the door. Before my daughter has taken off her tiny little coat I'm driving away in the car.

I don't listen to the radio. I don't talk to myself or roll down the windows. I try to relax in the silence of my solitary body, but all I can think about is the force of my hand coming down on her knee. I hit her, hard. For nothing at all. For being nearly three. I hit her because she doesn't know how to control herself, and I don't know how to let go.

I know how to tighten the cold hard fist of my heart.

I don't remember how to open it.

The small space of my car closes around me. The air grows hot and stale, and I can't breathe it in. My back sweats; my heart races. And just as I'm about to let the panic wash over me, I start screaming. It's not a scream that comes from my throat, or from my lungs, but a scream that comes from the shut place I carry inside me, a scream that could swell and swell without end. It's made of equal parts terror and rage, multiplied and multiplied by the silence of all these years.

. . .

By the time I get to work, I've composed myself again. I've cleaned the streaked mascara off my face and reapplied my lipstick. I don't tell my colleagues what has happened in the car: not about smacking my daughter's leg, not about the screaming. I teach a class. I meet with students. I eat lunch at my desk.

At the end of the day, I drive back to the preschool house to pick up my daughter. When I knock on the door, I can see she's just inside, waving to me, her mouth stretched open in a crooked, gap-toothed smile, her arms open and reaching toward me, her eyes open and shining with joy. The door opens and she throws herself into my arms. She holds nothing back.

With her head against my shoulder, the weight of her tiny body against my chest, I hold her tight and don't let go. I want nothing to break her. Not even me. Not ever. Not even a little.

. . .

In one dream I'm in a remote building: a garage or a barn or a basement. A place with corrugated metal walls and a very high ceiling. A shaft of light cuts through the rafters but has no source that I can see. I sit in a chair, unrestrained, watching as he feeds severed human forearms into a wood chipper. Afterward, he places a severed thigh on a table in front of me and begins to dissect it, slicing open the skin with a wheel-knife, pulling back the muscles and tendons with a pair of pliers and a fork. He has his back to me the whole time, so that I can see only the line of his body under his clothes, the cut of his hair, the faintest sliver of his cheek. Suddenly there's a knock at the door. We both turn toward the sound; he goes to answer it. He turns and leads a long line of people I barely know into the room: the teacher at my daughter's preschool, my dentist, the barista at my favorite coffee shop. I know what's coming before it comes. I do not cry out or try to tell him to stop.

I never say anything at all.

· · ·

I want to have another baby, I say. It's a Saturday afternoon. I've just put my daughter down for a nap in her bed. My Husband is planting a tree in the yard behind our house. He's hesitant. It's been only a few months since I came out of the depression from the first. *I've started a book,* I remind him, a task we both know keeps my mind from skittering away, *and I'll be nearly finished with it by the time the baby is born.* He makes me promise to find a therapist, *someone you can trust,* to prepare for what may follow out of the birth. *I want to be better,* I say. *I swear I am trying to be better.*

I tell The Newest Therapist that ten years ago I was kidnapped and raped by a man I knew. We're sitting in her office, a room with tall windows and creaky wooden floors in a converted Victorian house. A pair of plants hang from twin hooks near the windows. *But I don't want to talk about that,* I say.

Bullshit, she retorts. She asks for the two lists, and after reading the one I hand to her, after assuring me that I'm not remembering incorrectly, that I'm remembering exactly right, she suggests a few diagnoses for The Man I Used to Live With, and puts the DSM-IV in my hands. We talk about what may have drawn me to him in the first place, and about strategies for getting my anger and fear in check. We talk about the book I am writing, poems about growing up in the rural Midwest, and about the book we both know I must write after this.

. . .

When my son is born, the birth is peaceful: slow and calm and controlled. At the hospital, Mom holds one hand, tears welling behind her glasses; My Husband holds the other, cheering me on. Outside, in the waiting room, my sisters play board games with my daughter. Dad leads her up and down the hallways, to the bathroom, to the aquarium, to the cafeteria for a banana and juice.

Back in our home, days later, logs crackle in the fireplace while my daughter feeds her brand-new baby brother a bottle, holding his head so gently to her chest. They are both cradled in My Husband's arms; all three of them cuddling under a blanket at one end of the couch. I sit at the other end, only a little apart, taking pictures of the light glowing in their faces.

.   .   .

What do you feel in the dream, The Newest Therapist asks, *when you see him approaching?* She suggests a few quiet options: *Do you feel concerned? Or nervous? Or afraid?* I know she wants me to pin a name on the feeling. It's part of the process, the experts say, of becoming a whole person again, of weaving the traumatic event back into the fabric of memory. If I can name what I feel when he comes to kill me in my dreams, for instance—fear or fright or terror—maybe I can choose one name for what I felt when I saw him approaching me in the parking lot, or when he drove me around in circles in my car, or when he asked me to lie down on the mattress in the corner of the soundproof room.

But I do not feel fear, or fright, or terror. I did not feel concerned or nervous or afraid. There is no one word for it I can say. Because though I probably do feel something like fear and fright and terror, I also feel joy and ecstasy and relief. *He's finally come back. There's no more waiting,* I think.

.   .   .

When I'm awake I see him everywhere. The man who crosses the street not at the intersection, not when the signal says WALK, but up the way a bit, near the middle of the block. Or the man in the restaurant with his back to me: his long curls, the cheap watch, its fraying nylon strap. It's surprising how many strangers have his build, wear his clothes, stand with their feet spread wide apart, scratching the crease between neck and chin with the three middle fingers of either hand in the same arrogant way. Most of the time I recognize the impostor almost instantly because there is no feeling of being lowered by a rope very slowly, of my tongue turning to ash, to mud. I stop what I'm doing anyway and watch the stranger for a long long time.

. . .

I am out walking the dog one morning and stop for a moment at an intersection to lean over the stroller, to tickle my son's fat belly, and twist a tangle of his reddish curls around my finger. The dog perks up and takes aim at something behind us. I turn, see a man's large frame standing right behind me, and scream. Not a yelp, but a bloodcurdling horror-movie scream. A long moment passes before I realize that this stranger, who lives in my neighborhood probably, is waiting patiently for a chance to pass. The dog foams and growls and tries to lunge for the man as he walks around us without speaking.

. . .

In the afternoon I take my children to the park for a play-date. Two of my friends have invited us to join them; they each have a child the age of my son, and these children are happy to toddle around the jungle gym, climb up and down the ladders, and, only with tremendous encouragement, roll headfirst down the slide. I try to join the motherly conversation: the woes of finding day care, of keeping a part-time nanny, all the gear that must be schlepped to the doctor for a checkup only to return with a virus that causes diarrhea for days. My daughter follows her brother up the ladder a few dozen times before she declares that the babies are boring and bolts across the playground, where she asks a complete stranger to push her on the swings. He looks around, smiles at her benevolently, before giving her a little shove on the back.

She doesn't answer when I call her to come.

When she sees me finally pick up her brother and march toward the swings to retrieve her, she sprints to the sandpit, where she greets a scruffy-looking vagrant sleeping on the park bench. Just as I reach the sandpit, she bolts again, this time to the other side of the jungle gym where I can't see her, or anyone else she might be talking to. I apologize to my friends, put my son in the stroller, chase my daughter down, and leave.

Before we get to the car, before I've buckled the children into their seats and locked the doors, my voice has grown so loud and terrible that it frightens even me.

You don't understand, I say, my voice hoarse and rattling in my chest. *The world is not the kind of safe place you think it is.* Her hands squirm in my hands. She searches my face, trying to understand. *There are people who would do terrible things to you. People who would take you and kill you and I would never ever see you again.*

Before I'm finished saying this, she cries out: *Mommy, you're scaring me!*

You should be scared, I say, starting the car.

· · ·

The worst dream goes like this: I am stuck in a single point, unable to move, while the world goes on at normal speed around me. I can't open my eyes fully because the light is too bright. I can't move my limbs, which are stuck in molasses, maybe, or made of molasses. Time, too, is sticky and slow. No particular danger threatens me, but I panic anyway. Nearby, a group of children squeal and giggle and run. A couple passes, holding hands, bread-and-buttering around me. They take no notice of me at all. A bus unloads its passengers. A tree drops acorns on the grass. The day is sunny and warm.

· · ·

On my very best days, my children and I take turns cartwheeling through the yard. We finger-paint long rolls of paper on the floor under the dining room table before I chase them through the house with messy fingers; they squeal, running, paint on their faces and bellies and armpits, and we are all laughing, laughing, laughing. We hold hands and jump through the sprinkler, each of us fully dressed, soaking wet. Or we pack a picnic and ride our bicycles to the playground, where we spread a blanket and eat cross-legged on the ground, or lying on our sides, or crawling like lions in circles. That afternoon we might fall asleep together in the bed, the grass blades still stuck in our hair. While I make dinner, we turn up the music and dance in the kitchen and I swing my daughter back and forth, back and forth singing, *I know one thing: that I love you.*

I love you I love you I love you.

And it's true, so true, that suddenly I've got tears running down my face, so I put her down to find a towel, a tissue, any scrap will do. She pulls at my sweater. *I just need a minute,* I say, turning away. But then they're both pulling at my sweater, their hands on my skirt, my legs. *I just need a minute. Just a minute!* I say. But then I'm already checking the soup, or sweeping the floor, or putting the dishes away. My son lies down on the floor, deflated. My daughter storms toward her room. They know it's too late. A door has closed. I'm gone.

. . .

I wake in a cold sweat, crying out in pain. The father of my children wakes or does not wake. He rubs my back, rolls over, toward me, and invites me into the nook between his arm and torso. *It's real pain I'm feeling,* I want to tell him, though I couldn't point to any one place it most hurts.

I climb from the bed and weave my way through the house checking all the locks on the doors, peering out the blinds of the windows, my skin prickling, my hair standing on end. I pour a glass of water in the kitchen, and think of taking the longest, sharpest knife out of the drawer before I crawl back into bed. I might watch the darkness through one open eye for hours before I close it and sleep.

I open the door and enter the room where my children are sleeping. I stand between them, listening to their bubbles and hiccups, their slow steady breathing. I rest my palm on my son's back, his cool cotton pajamas, and underneath, his dream-warm skin. I smooth back the damp line of my daughter's hair with the corner of my thumb. I lean down to kiss her cheek, and inhale the smell that belongs to her and no other. She looks so beautiful like this: her eyes closed, her mouth slightly open.

It all seems so fragile, this life that I have.

But no, I take it back.

This is the place I would point to.

This, right here, is the one place it most hurts.

[twelve]

ONCE, WHEN DAD drank two beers at dinner, he insisted I've been writing poems since kindergarten. I have no memory of this. My first memory of writing is in fourth grade. While my classmates write expository sentences in cursive, I am writing a novel. Or that's what I call it, anyway. A thinly veiled excuse to imagine myself caught in a love triangle with two of my real-life friends. We travel to a cabin in the Colorado mountains. The other girl goes missing. *Finally, we're alone.* I have not yet been to the Colorado mountains, but imagine them steep, sloped, snowy, and thick with trees. I imagine they are dangerous. I show the novel to my teacher, my librarian, my friends, my parents. I offer all the handwritten pages, eager for their praise.

By my first year of high school, I start keeping a journal: a spiral notebook in which I write everything I can't say out loud. I show it to no one; no one knows I write each night before I go to bed. The notebook stays secret for years, until Dad finds it left haphazardly in the basement. He hands the notebook over to my mother, who calls me into the bathroom. She grills me about the material, *this smut, this garbage.* I stay silent and nod or shake my head. She wants to know if I am a virgin. I swear that I am. This is a bold-faced lie. A year earlier I was raped by a drunk boy in my friend's basement.

I don't write that in my notebook.

I write about sneaking out of the house to get drunk, smoke pot, and have sex with boys who have already graduated from high school. I write about fucking a grown man on the golf course in the middle of the night. How his cock is so large it nearly splits me in two. I write about the man who dances me into a corner at a party and fucks me in the front seat of his car. I write about the college student who fucks me on the bottom bunk at a frat party, my head spinning from the alcohol, my friend passed out in the next room. I write about going to apartments to give head. In my notebook, it's all I want, this fucking.

Mom stands in the bathroom, the notebook in one hand, her other hand on her hip. She's angry but her voice is a whisper. *What have you done?* Sitting on the edge of the sink, I say, *It's fiction, Mom. My way of dealing.* A lie, and she believes me. She gives me back the notebook and it never comes up again.

. . .

I'm cleaning my office when I stumble across a stack of my early poems stapled together, stuffed into a magazine file of my writing from college. I'm not even sure I want to read them, afraid I'll find something new I've forgotten: a broken bone, a fist-sized bruise.

Instead, I find delicate, trite little verses about The Man I Live With: how his touch, his gaze, his whispers in my ear wake me from a dream I didn't know I was having. In these poems, my love transforms me: it's beautiful, transcendent, sublime. The poems are terrible, but I remember feeling so proud of them, folding copies into envelopes and submitting them to magazines, printing and stapling a whole packet and pushing it across a table toward a kind and generous teacher. I remember showing one poem to The Man I Live With, who grows so angry as he's reading that he tears the page into pieces that fall to the floor. *You don't get to write about me,* he insists.

. . .

There's the story I have, and the story he has, and there is a story the police have in Evidence. There's the story the journalist wrote for the paper. There's the story The Female Officer filed in her report; her story is not my story. There's the story he must have told his mother when he called her on the phone; there's the story she must have told herself. There's the story you'll have after you put down this book. It's an endless network of stories. This story tells me who I am. It gives me meaning. And I want to mean something so badly.

. . .

The first poem I ever publish appears in an undergraduate literary journal a few months after I graduate, after the kidnapping. I'm invited to read at the issue launch party, where a single microphone stands in a little clearing in the corner of a dark restaurant. Months earlier I sat at a table in this same spot, eating dinner with The Man I Live With, who was angry about one thing or another, calling me a cunt while I cried into my soup. I'm the second reader, or maybe the third, so nervous that the paper flutters like an animal in my hand. I'm standing under a spotlight, sweating through my shirt, my voice cracking every few syllables:

> I can feel you
> in the back of my throat.
> In the place I begin
> the word "god."

I've practiced in front of the mirror at home every morning for weeks. My professors, teachers, My Good Friend, and an ex-lover sit in the audience, all of them veiled in shadow. It's better that I can't see their faces.

. . .

In graduate school I begin trying, in earnest, to write. I write about anything but The Man I Used to Live With—the seasons, my mother and father, protofeminism in neglected epistolary novels from the early modern period, the Spanish Civil War—but it always comes back to him, to all that happened. I try to write about My First Husband who sleeps on the couch watching NASCAR while I sit at my desk blowing smoke out the window; instead I write about the dreams, the pills, the swarm of gnats mating outside the screen. It's the only thing that pulls me out of bed: these poems that lie and misdirect, that circle and circle all the things I can't say out loud. Each day I begin writing, I think, *This is it. Today is the day.* As if typing anything other than that unthinkable thing were a kind of breaking free. Each day, as I'm sitting at my computer, watching the words accumulate on the page, I feel elated, euphoric. *Look at how far I've come,* I think. *How far these words can carry me.*

· · ·

After I graduate from that writing program and enter the prestigious one in Texas; after I write my dissertation and earn a PhD; after I have written and published my first book, I begin trying to write this one. The story I must tell.

I try to write in the daytime, sitting at my desk, or on the couch, or reclining in the bed, while my daughter is at school and my son naps in his crib. I try to write about The Man I Used to Live With, about all that happened, but instead I write about addiction, or my children, or the dreams. I say, *I can't write with all these distractions. All these interruptions make it impossible to think.*

I try to write at night, while the children sleep in their beds, while their father sits beside me on the couch or reclines on the pillow next to mine, his own computer propped open on his lap; instead I shop for houses we can't afford, clothes I will not buy, vacations we will not take. I say, *Maybe if I could just get away for a while, if only I could have a little time and space to think,* and I apply for an artist residency in upstate New York, where the windows of my studio look out to the green edge of a rolling mountain range, the tall grass licking at the trees.

The first day, the day I begin writing this book, I sit at the computer, in front of the window, my eyes on the grass, my fingers on the keys, and tears stream down my cheeks. I down whole glasses of scotch and crawl under the desk.

After dinner, I call home from my computer and watch the small lithe bodies of my children tangle over My Husband, who tries, in earnest, to talk about his day while they whine or cry or paw at him or the image they're seeing of me. It's past their bedtime and they need to go to sleep. I say, *I love you. I miss you.* And mean it. And they say, *Please come home.* I blow a kiss and My Husband mouths the words: *Are you okay?* And I say, *No, not at all, actually.* I want to come home. I want the tangle of their bodies in my lap. I need that. I need My Husband's breath in my hair before I drift off to sleep. Their love is all that saves me from the dreams.

After we hang up, there is only silence. There's only darkness lapping at the window. There's only an empty page on the screen.

Only the story can bridge it.

.   .   .

The funny version of the story goes like this: a long time ago in a galaxy far, far away . . . I was kidnapped and raped by a man I used to live with. I'm kind of fucked up about it.

It's not a joke I tell at parties.

Most of the time I don't tell the story at all. Whole close friendships have come and gone or continue to this day and I haven't breathed a word.

Other times it takes only one glass of wine and I'm spilling the beans to near strangers. Or it doesn't take wine. Maybe it's ten in the morning. A new friend tells me a secret. I tell mine. It's usually the same reaction: first there's shock, a hand over the mouth or to the chest, always *I'm so sorry.*

I'm the one who's sorry. I'm sorry I keep telling this story.

.   .   .

Here is the shortest version: for five hours on July 5, 2000, I was held prisoner in a soundproof room in a basement apartment rented for the sole purpose of raping and killing me.

I could also say I lived with my kidnapper for two and a half years, and during all the time we lived together he didn't call it rape but fucking. When I finally moved out, he thought it would take only a few days of good, hard fucking to convince me to come home. If I refused, he planned to shoot me in the cunt and then the head.

His words, not mine.

. . .

I'm afraid the story isn't finished happening.

Sometimes I think there is no entirely true story I could tell. Because there are some things I just don't know, and other things I just can't say. Which is not a failure of memory but of language.

. . .

If people ask what my book is about I do not say it is about the time I was kidnapped and raped by a man I used to live with. That level of honesty borders on rude. It is against the rules of polite society to admit having been raped to a near stranger. I change the subject. I point to the sky and say, *Oh look, a flock of turtles!* Or I ask the near stranger whether he thinks the housing market has finally turned around.

Should I buy stock now or wait until closer to retirement? This is usually enough to get him off the scent.

To my acquaintances I say I'm writing about violence and memory and the body. Or I say it's about violence and desire. I say I'm writing about a traumatic event in my past. Most people understand this as code for *Think long and hard before asking more questions about this.* Together we observe half a moment of silence before my acquaintance cocks his head back the slightest bit and opens his mouth to say, *Ah . . . I see.*

. . .

In the story I have, I am always escaping, always moving from one place to another, or standing still where there is nothing to do with my hands, and everywhere, in all of it, the walls are high, covered in thick blue Styrofoam, the ceiling out of reach. I might turn the corner and stumble into terror or love or loss. The story does have seasons. There's the breeze of hands up Sunday's dress, the bruise, the blue skirt I left. There's the lure of infinite sleep. A sea route. A route down the river. The story I have is a map for this place, which has no actual location, no axes of orientation. In which direction do I travel today? Away and back. Away and back. Over and over. Am I not endlessly circling? Have I not been here before? This temple. This harbor. There is no outside, no inside. Am I not close to the center? Here is the forest. The fog. The last leaf slipping, the rub of my thumb and finger. And, like that: it's gone.

. . .

I admit to My Husband that I'm afraid to post a schedule of my upcoming readings on my website. He sighs, closes his laptop, and turns to me. *What do you think is going to happen?* he asks. *I think he's going to show up and shoot me with a gun,* I say. He sighs harder.

It's not the only outcome I imagine. Sometimes I imagine he is dead. Or he is still alive, barely eking out a living in Venezuela. He loves another woman, I imagine. Or he has murdered her. Or he is not in Venezuela, but is lying low in the States, waiting for me to show him where to find me. And when he does, I imagine the ways I will struggle, how I will open the door to run. I imagine what I would give him in exchange for the lives of My Husband and our children.

There is nothing I would not give him.

. . .

The story becomes the mind's protection. The story becomes the mind's defense. An apology. A collection of excuses. A set of forgivable lies. As when my children come to me for affection and I give them something to eat. Or a fresh shirt. Or I busy myself with sweeping the floor and making the beds. *I don't have time for this,* I say.

But I do have time. There's nothing stopping me. Not really.

To My Husband I say, *I'm too far gone. I don't know how to love.* We might be standing on opposite sides of the island in the kitchen. I might be pouring him a glass of wine or stirring a vegetable stew. *I'm trapped on the other side of a wide, dark chasm,* I say. I might break down in tears. He holds out his arms, but I cover my face, look down, turn away.

In this story, I'm always turning away.

. . .

My daughter asks what I do while she's at school all day and I tell her anything but the truth. *I'm working. I'm reading. I'm teaching,* I say. But the truth is: sometimes I put my head against the table or the desk or the cool edge of the toilet. I puke, or scream, or pull my hair out in handfuls, and I weep. The blood rises to my face until it feels like his hand is here, right here, squeezing, squeezing. He is spitting into my face, kneeling on my chest, heavy as a pile of stones. *He will kill me for this,* I think.

But I don't stop writing. I cover the screen and type without looking at the words. I crawl into my bed and pull the covers up over my body, over the computer, up over my head. *This cave of making.* It's the last place he'd think to look.

By the time I pick my children up from school, I've cleaned the streaked mascara off my face and reapplied my lipstick. At home, I play with my son on the floor. I make dinner. Or if I do not make dinner, we order pizza and the four of us eat in the living room watching an animated movie. We take walks and work in the yard on the weekends. From the outside it all appears very normal.

· · ·

My girlfriend asks how this book is going and I say, *I'm sooooo ready to be done. It's not fun to write this, you know.* She picks at the tip of her straw, or fingers the arch of her eyebrow, and tells me that my children will someday feel lucky to have this book. We might be sitting on her porch or at a picnic table in the park or the only outside table at a restaurant. I say, *This will be the last version of the story I ever tell.* I know how ridiculous this sounds. How foolish. How naive. Because the truth is: I'm afraid of what will happen when it's done. *I'm trapped,* I say. A prison I've built with this story. *I don't know how to escape it,* I say.

But I do know.

The story is a trap, a puzzle, a paradox.

Ending it creates a door.

[thirteen]

MY BODY IS cold and naked and shaking as he tightens the nuts on the thick steel U-bolts anchoring my arms to the chair. The whole time he's tying my ankle to a four-by-four with a thick leather belt, he's talking about his assault rifle in the hallway, about dynamite in the walls, and how he'll blow up the building if the police come. He doesn't notice that I'm flexing every muscle in my leg to give myself wiggle room inside his leather belt.

Once I'm secured, he goes into the other room and brings back a camera. *See? I'll be watching you, even if you can't see me, even if I'm not in the room.*

He puts a choke-chain collar around my neck—the kind you might use to train an unruly dog—and hooks the free end to the back of the chair.

He turns up the radio, calls it *white noise*, his mouth close to my ear. He explains this term, as if he's just invented it. As if he's the first person who thought of saying it.

· · ·

He stands in front of me, between the chair and the mattress, tucking in his shirt, zipping up his pants, tying back his hair with a black rubber band. He puts his hands on his hips, pausing to take it all in.

I can't cover myself, or hide, or turn away.

. . .

Blood drips between my legs and into the bucket underneath my seat.

He laughs a little.

He says, if only I hadn't treated him so cruelly.

He says he's going out to get a drink at the bar, so that people can see him out and about, so he can establish an alibi. A story, he explains, about where he was, what he was doing when I died. *The next time I see you,* he says, *I'll shoot you in the cunt and then the head.*

He asks if I will love him forever.

. . .

He puts a pair of noise-canceling headphones over my ears. He puts the duct-taped glasses back on my face.

I hear the blood in my veins, the faintest murmur of sound from the radio. I see the black back of the glasses, a sliver of his shadow out the edges.

He kisses me sloppily, his hand fondling my naked breast,

pinching my nipple, then drifting down across my stomach to ruffle the upper line of my pubic hair.

He clears his throat, and closes himself behind the door.

. . .

I bend my head to look—*how much blood?*—and the head-phones slide down my face and into my lap. My body is shaking so hard; it's hard to catch my breath.

The assault rifle leans against the wall in the hallway: I remember how he kept it in one corner of his closet, under the striped sweaters, the cotton briefs, those stupid Hawaiian shirts, always unbuttoned and hanging over one shoulder, his pants pulled to his knees, his fingers moistened with spit.

I shake the thought out of my head; the glasses go bouncing to the floor. The room comes slowly into focus. He'll come rushing back in at any moment. He'll shoot me in the cunt and then in the face, or the ear, or underneath my chin, my hair spattered across the soundproofed ceiling, the carpet, the door.

I wring my arm to see how the thick steel U-bolt around my wrist attaches to the chair: a two-inch galvanized fencing staple hammered deep into the wood.

I look around the room for the camera. I don't see one mounted anywhere. Not on the floor. Or by the door. Not on the back of the chair. The radio blares a song I know: *White noise*, he said. *White of forgetfulness. White of safety.*

. . .

I lean my head back against the chair and look at the ceiling, how the thick blue Styrofoam will look when the police find the crime scene. They'll load the pieces of my dead body into a black bag, haul it down the hallway, through the living room, and out to the parking lot, where newscasters with solemn faces will report the story. The bullets that entered my body. Our two names linked this way forever in the headlines.

. . .

But that story is not my story, I tell myself as I wiggle and twist and pull my foot out of the loose leather belt binding my leg to the chair. I lift it onto the seat and underneath my body.

Holding my breath, I pull my arm upward while I push against the seat with my foot. It hurts, this pulling: steel against skin against bone. My arm could break. The possibility of that makes me certain it won't.

I take a breath, pull my arm upward, upward, upward. The skin on my wrist blooms like a flower.

. . .

I feel the breath burning in my chest, the pressure of the leather against my ankle, the muscles in my foot on the seat lifting me upward, upward, upward.

I feel my elbow pushing down against the wood, my fingernails scratching tracks through the wood.

I feel the steel like a hinge against the arm I rock back and forth, the steel I pull left and right.

I feel the arm; I pull and force it upward, upward, always upward.

I feel the arm I tear unbolted.

. . .

I unscrew the nuts bolting my other arm to the chair. My fingers do not fumble, not once. The movements of my body are intentional and deliberate and precise.

I untie the rope around my other leg.

I unhook the chain around my neck from the chair.

I stand up straight and tall.

I wipe the blood spilling from my body with a tissue I drop beside the mattress before crossing the room to where my clothes lie in a neatly folded pile. I dress fast, stepping back toward the chair, where I pry the loosest two-by-four from the seat.

. . .

I hold the board above my head, ready to bash his skull loose as I twist the doorknob. It's unlocked.

My legs carry me into the dark hallway, through the dark living room, toward the windows, the blinds pulled closed. Even in the shadows I spot my keys on a table, the green and white beads of the lizard key ring, tossed into a pile of empty shopping bags, empty cardboard cups, empty boxes of screws and nails.

I lift the chain from my neck, over my head, let it rattle to the floor.

.   .   .

In the pulse of silence that follows, a story begins unfolding. Where it may take me, whether it will end here, I don't know. I don't need to. Because in this moment, when I'm alone in the darkness, all I am and was and ever will be is gathered up inside me. And every last bit of it urges me on.

And on.

And on.

I reach for the door. It's here. It's opening.

notes

from one

Page 3: *The clock's arms both point to eleven.* According to police reports, I actually entered the station at 10:06 PM. At 10:40 PM, The Female Officer transported me to the apartment building, where she observed a white car tarp lying in the gravel parking lot in front of the apartment. The Female Officer noticed that the door was open. She approached the apartment, knocked on the screen door, and announced herself as a police officer. She could hear music but no one would come to her call. Two other officers secured the area while The Female Officer transported me to the hospital for a sexual assault exam. When the search warrant was issued at 3:22 AM, detectives entered the building and began cataloging the evidence. The following morning, they applied for an arrest warrant on the charges of kidnapping, felonious restraint, forcible rape, and forcible sodomy.

from two

Page 13: *Schrödinger's famous thought experiment.* I admit that my account here is a dramatic oversimplification.

As Emma Komlos-Hrobsky, assistant editor at Tin House, has pointed out to me, a more accurate description of the paradox would involve saying that the equations we use to calculate the behavior of quantum particles suggest that the single atom of radioactive substance in this experiment enters a state of quantum superposition; that is, the psi function of the entire system contains in it an atom that both has and has not decayed, and poison that is and isn't released, and a cat that is and isn't dead. Schrödinger's point here is to illustrate that atomic indeterminacy doesn't translate particularly well to the macroscopic world. Unlike the atom, which can, at least theoretically, exist in a "blurred model" of reality, the cat can't be both alive and dead, because the act of observation forces the cat into one state or the other: the cat can be only either living or dead. See "The Present Situation in Quantum Mechanics: A Translation of Schrödinger's 'Cat Paradox'" in *Proceedings of the American Philosophical Society,* 124, no. 5 (1980): 323–338. John D. Trimmer, translator.

Page 15: *Like something I memorized long ago.* On the one hand, neuroscientists say that traumatic memories degrade at the same rate as other kinds of memories. One study on memory stability asked participants to describe the memory of hearing about the attack on the World Trade Center on September 11, 2001, and also to describe a memory from the day before the attack. Years later researchers asked again: tell us about the day before the attack, tell us about the attack. Both sets of memories showed the same degree of narrative drift.

On the other hand, psychologists say traumatic memories don't change. Even from the moment of the trauma, the mind engages mechanisms of avoidance and denial in order to isolate and quarantine the memory of trauma. The result of this is that the traumatic memory withdraws from conscious recollection and migrates to the memory of the lived body, where it might reemerge, perfectly preserved, at any time.

Page 17: *My Handsome Friend*. After reading about my friend's fear in the police reports, I write to him to apologize. *I never knew that had happened to you, and I'm so so so sorry. Sorry doesn't cover it actually.* My friend writes back, offers an apology of his own, admitting maybe he wasn't really there for me in the ways I needed him. *The thought that keeps me going when I remember all of that,* he writes, *is that you and I both have families . . . and we are both leading fuller, happier lives than that a-hole ever even dreamed of . . .*

from three

Page 27: *It all starts like this.* See Charles M. Anderson's "Suture, Stigma, and the Pages That Heal" in *Writing and*

Healing: Toward an Informed Practice, Charles M. Anderson and Marian M. MacCurdy, editors, for a discussion of the ways in which subjectivity is created, positioned, and controlled by our participation in the story networks and discourses of the other. Although, as Jacques Lacan has suggested, this participation gives us access to discursive and narrative meaning, it's not without cost: "Self and all that murky term might or might not mean, is compromised, some have said, to the point of disappearance. To participate in the discourse of the other is necessarily to suffer the loss of self and to be, in a very real sense, written over or spoken out of existence" (Anderson 60).

Page 33: *This is what he wants.* See Simone de Beauvoir, *The Second Sex*:

> We have seen that in a majority of women a passive sexuality has also developed since childhood: woman likes to be embraced, caressed, and especially after puberty she wants to be flesh in a man's arms; the role of subject is normally assigned to him; she knows that; she has been told repeatedly "a man has no need of being good-looking"; she is not supposed to look for the inert qualities of an object in him, but for strength and virile power.

Page 33: *The body remembers.* See Sabine C. Koch et al., eds., *Body Memory, Metaphor and Movement*; Maurice

Merleau-Ponty, *Phenomenology of Perception*; Pierre Bour-
dieu, "Structures, *Habitus*, Practices" in *The Logic of Practice*.

Page 38: *He calls me Puta! Chingada!* Octavio Paz, writing
in *The Labyrinth of Solitude* about gender coding in Mexico,
defines this term, *chingar*, which means to *injure, to lacerate,
to violate*; Paz writes:

> The verb is masculine, active, cruel: it stings, wounds,
> gashes, stains. And it provokes a bitter, resentful satis-
> faction. The person who suffers this action is passive,
> inert and open, in contrast to the active, aggressive and
> closed person who inflicts it. The *chingón* is the *macho*,
> the male; he rips open the *chingada*, the female, who
> is pure passivity, defenseless against the exterior world
> (77).

The term's deep history can be traced back to the Spanish
conquest of Mexico, to La Malinche, a Nahua woman who
translated for Hernán Cortés, who bore him a child, who
helped him enslave and annihilate the entire Aztec Empire.
To the Spanish she was known as Doña Marina, a helpful,
obedient woman. But over time, especially among Mexican
nationalists, her name became synonymous with treachery;
to this day the term *malinchista* refers to a disloyal Mexican.
In popular folklore, she is often placed in stark opposi-
tion to chaste women: Mary, mother of Jesus, the Virgin

of Guadalupe. More recently, she has become known as *La Chingada*, the woman who is fucked.

Page 42: *Another memory comes back.* In normal everyday situations, the brain turns experience (impressions, perceptions, observations) into information, which is encoded for processing and temporarily stored. Synaptic consolidation, the first step toward making experience a memory, begins with a series of cascading changes and communications between and among molecules, triggering protein reactions and changes in genetic information and gene expression, which in turn leads to the permanent alteration of certain synaptic proteins in the brain. All of this takes place within the first few minutes or hours of an experience. System consolidation, on the other hand, takes up to two decades, and involves the gradual process of reorganizing and transporting the memories, temporarily stored in one part of the brain, to another part of the brain where the memories can be stored more permanently.

In traumatic experiences, however, stress hormones trigger a significant narrowing of consciousness, which means there is increased memory retention for certain details, and partial or total amnesia for others. This altered memory gets passed throughout the brain where it is processed differently from other memories by using much more synaptic energy and requiring that the energy be distributed across many more encoding neurons. This makes the traumatic memory more engorged with sensation and perception than other memories, which means it gets consolidated differently. Or, in some cases, the traumatic memory may not be consolidated at all. Because the traumatic memory often does not fit into the flow and structure of linear time and narrative, it may detach from normal events and memory. This detachment can take many forms, including event-specific amnesia, which may last for hours, weeks, or years; dissociation, which refers to a compartmentalization and fracturing of experience; or the memory may completely lack a semantic component, which is to say, it can't be spoken. Without a narrative, the traumatic memory splits off from ordinary consciousness, and elements of the trauma may begin to intrude into consciousness; as terrifying perceptions, obsessional preoccupations, and anxiety reactions. Without a narrative, the experience cannot be fully absorbed by consciousness, which is not to say it is not remembered, but that the memory enters a liminal realm in which it is both acknowledged and unacknowledged, consolidated and not consolidated, part of you and not part, perhaps even indefinitely. See Pierre Janet (1919, 1925), and Bessel A. van der Kolk and Rita Fisler (1995) for a detailed discussion of the relationship between trauma, dissociation, and memory consolidation.

from four

Page 45: *Two armless chairs face one another.* Samuel Beckett, *Ohio Impromptu.* The actual line in the stage direction reads: *Two plain armless white deal chairs.*

Page 46: *He wants me to achieve mental balance.* The official diagnosis, as I understand it, is post-traumatic stress disorder (PTSD), which, in 2000, was still a relatively "new" category of mental disorder. This particular diagnosis first appears in the DSM-III (1980), which includes 265 diagnostic categories, 82 of which did not appear in the DSM-II. As one of the "new" diagnoses, PTSD is classified as a subcategory of anxiety disorders, a stress response precipitated by a catastrophically traumatic event that is *outside the range of usual human experience.* This particular diagnosis initially evolved as the result of the combined efforts of researchers, social workers, and psychiatrists to describe a combination of symptoms particular to combat veterans, and its inclusion in the DSM-III is considered a watershed event. Whereas "shell shock" had long been considered a weakness of the individual to handle the rigors of war, for the first time experts seemed to agree that a stress response was not the result of a defect in the individual, but rather a normal reaction to an abnormal experience. Over time, mental health professionals began to remark on similarities between the symptoms manifested by combat veterans and those manifested by Holocaust survivors, civilian victims of war, abused children, and raped and battered women. Eventually, researchers began to say that traumatic events might be so endemic and pervasive that catastrophic trauma isn't really outside of the realm of normal human experience at all.

Page 49: *The sunlight lynched in the blinds.* Lucie Brock-Broido, "How Can It Be I Am No Longer I." The lines read:

> . . . How flinching
> The world will seem—in the lynch
> Of light as I sail home in a winter steeled
> For the deaths of the few loved left living I will
> Always love.

Page 54: *Even though they're more troubling to look at.* See Susan Sontag, *On Photography*:

> To suffer is one thing; another thing is living with the photographed images of suffering, which does not necessarily strengthen conscience and the ability to be compassionate. It can also corrupt them. Once one has seen such images, one has started down the road of seeing more—and more. Images transfix. Images anesthetize.

from five

Page 59: *How is it possible to reclaim the body.* See Maurice Merleau-Ponty, "Eye and Mind," the last essay he published before his death:

> The mirror emerges because I am a visible see-er, because there is a reflexivity of the sensible; the mirror translates and reproduces that reflexivity. In it, my externality becomes complete. Everything that is most secret about me passes into that face, that flat, closed being of which I was already dimly aware, from having seen my reflection mirrored in water.

Page 62: *It's the kind of job a girl like me has spent her whole life training for.* See Mary Wollstonecraft, *A Vindication of the Rights of Women*, especially chapter three, "The Same Subject Continued": *Taught from their infancy that beauty is woman's sceptre, the mind shapes itself to the body, and, roaming round its gilt cage, only seeks to adorn its prison.*

Page 63: *Everyone in the club gets to see.* In "The Sexual Aberrations," collected in *Three Essays on the Theory of Sexuality*, Freud argues that the "history of human civilization shows beyond any doubt that there is an intimate connection between cruelty and the sexual instinct." The connection is so intimate that "the sexuality of most male human beings contains an element of aggressiveness—a desire to subjugate; the biological significance of it seems to lie in the need for overcoming the resistance of the sexual object by means other than the process of wooing."

Page 63: *That image, of the self.* John Berger, *Ways of Seeing.* Also Gilles Deleuze and Félix Guattari, *Anti-Oedipus* and *A Thousand Plateaus.*

Page 64: *I cry out each time in pain or mock pain.* See Naomi Wolf, *The Beauty Myth*: "If a woman's sexual sense of self has centered on pain as far back as the record goes, who is she without it? If suffering is beauty and beauty is love, she cannot be sure she will be loved if she does not suffer. It is hard, because of such conditioning, to envisage a female body free of pain and still desirable."

Page 65: *Which is certainly not . . . I meant to become.* Denis Johnson, "The White Fires of Venus":

I'm telling you it's cold inside the body that is not the body,
lonesome behind the face
that is certainly not the face
of the person one meant to become.

from six

Page 74: *It's possible I'm not remembering right.* Memory, in this case, means not only the power of the mind to remember things, but also the mind itself, insofar as it is regarded as the total sum of things remembered. By *memory* I do not necessarily mean any specific recollection, remembrance, impression, or reminiscence, but rather the relationship or association among impressions, sensory perceptions, and thoughts that arise out of lived experience. That is to say, human memory is relational, and fallible, and is not so much an accurate accounting of events as it is a set of processes by which we encode, store, and retrieve information. These processes depend on reinforcement, which moves the memory relationship from short-lived categories (immediate memory, working memory) to longer-lasting ones (long-term memory) by bringing together certain sensory information and discarding other information. The main feature of this process, of converting short-term information to long-term memory for storage, is loss, the forgetting of distracting information. It is no coincidence, then, that the word itself, *memory*, comes from the Anglo-French *memorie*, something written to be kept in mind; from the Latin *memoria*, a reminiscence; from the Old Norse, *Mímir*, the name of the giant who guards the Well of Wisdom; and from the Old English *murnan*, to mourn.

Page 77: *Slouching toward oblivion.* W. B. Yeats, "The Second Coming":

> And what rough beast, its hour come round at last,
> Slouches towards Bethlehem to be born?

Page 79: *Do not refute who I am!* Paul Celan, "O little root of a dream":

> even
> here,
> where you
> refute me,
> to the letter.

Page 86: *I look over my shoulder and see him.* Michel Foucault discusses the relationship between spectacle and surveillance and power in "Panopticism":

> He who is subjected to a field of visibility, and who knows it, assumes responsibility for the constraints of power; he makes them play spontaneously upon himself; he inscribes in himself the power relation in which he simultaneously plays both roles; he becomes the principle of his own subjugation.

from seven

Page 91: *As if relief might flow from unfamiliarity.* Samuel Beckett, *Ohio Impromptu:* "Relief he had hoped would flow from unfamiliarity."

from eight

Page 112: *At first, I have a body.* Anthony Synnott, "Tomb, Temple, Machine and Self: The Social Construction of the Body":

Plato believed the body was a "tomb," Paul said it was the "temple" of the Holy Spirit, the Stoic philosopher Epictetus taught that it was a "corpse." Christians believed, and believe, that the body is not only physical, but also spiritual and mystical, and many believed it was an allegory of church, state and family. Some said it was cosmic: one with the planets and the constellations. Descartes wrote that the body is a "machine," and this definition has underpinned biomedicine to this day; but Sartre said that the body is the self.

from **nine**

Page 119: *All I want is someone to fuck me senseless.* The headline of a recent article by Katie Roiphe in *Newsweek* announces, "Spanking Goes Mainstream: From the steamy bestseller *Fifty Shades of Grey* to HBO's *Girls*, sexual domination is in vogue. Katie Roiphe on why women's power at work may be fueling the craze." Roiphe quips, "Even though fantasies are something that, by definition, one can't control, they seem to be saying something about modern women that nearly everyone wishes wasn't said."

from **ten**

Page 129: *In a variation of Schrödinger's famous thought experiment.* My description is, again, admittedly, a drastic oversimplification, this time of the work of noted quantum theorists Hans Moravec, Bruno Marchal, and Max Tegmark. See Wikipedia, "Quantum Suicide and Immortality."

Page 134: *I wish you all the best.* This e-mail, dated October 31, 2007, begins like this:

Hi,
I'm sorry to bother you with this message. I'm sure the last thing you want to be remembered of is our whole

break-up [. . .] though it's sad that that one incident probably erased in your memory and for sure overshadows the wonderful almost storybook time we had together for three years, traveling through Europe and Mexico, and well you were there, you know what we had.

Years later, I finally respond to him—*You better run, motherfucker*—but the message comes back as undeliverable.

Page 137: *What was the word there for silence?* In "October," Louise Glück writes:

> I can't hear your voice
> for the wind's cries, whistling over the bare ground
>
> I no longer care
> what sound it makes
>
> when was I silenced, when did it first seem
> pointless to describe that sound
>
> what it sounds like can't change what it is—

Page 137: *In the transcript of the Venezuelan extradition trial.* Translated by the author from the Spanish.

from eleven

Page 160: *You should be scared.* James Boswell, writing for *London Magazine* in 1777, offers this:

> Of all the sufferings to which the mind of man is liable in
> this state of darkness and imperfection, the passion of fear
> is the severest, excepting the remorse of a guilty conscience,
> which however has much of fear in it, being not solely a
> tormenting anguish of reflection on the past, but a direful
> foreboding of the future; or as the sacred scriptures strong-
> ly express it, "a certain fearful looking for of judgement."

from twelve

Page 165: *I write everything I can't say out loud.* One of my
students at my first-ever real job is a doctoral candidate in
the Child Language Acquisition Program. I ask her about
what I understand to be the links between memory and
narrative. She tells me about Genie, a girl who was kept in
such isolation by her parents that she never learned to talk.
For most of her early life she was locked in a room and tied
to a potty chair; thus restrained, she was forced to sit alone
day after day, and often through the night. She was discovered in 1970 at the age of thirteen, uttering only infantile
gurgles, wearing only a diaper.

A team of researchers worked with Genie for years, and they eventually taught her a few simple words. She could communicate her needs and desires through gestures and ungrammatical phrases, but could not form sentences. My student explains that this case reinforces the theory that we're born with the principles of language hardwired into our genes but that there is also a deadline for learning them. If a first language isn't acquired by puberty, the theory goes, it won't be acquired at all.

My student tells me about Genie because though she lacked language, and had no chance of acquiring it, she found ways to describe her experience. When researchers tried to elicit memories of Genie's past—such as where she was sitting when she used to eat cereal—Genie could respond with language—*In the pot,* she'd say. It was clear that these memories distressed her, but more importantly, it was also clear she could use recently acquired language to describe events that had happened before words were a part of her world. The events were not integrated into a narrative but constituted memory just the same.

Unfortunately, my student tells me, the story did not end well for Genie. When the research grants gave out, the researchers working on the case abandoned her, and while some believed she could have continued to learn, others dismissed her as "mentally retarded" (their term), at least functionally. For a while, she returned to live with her mother, who quickly found she was incapable of caring for the girl.

For years she was passed from foster house to foster house, where she was abused, beaten, ridiculed, eventually finding her way to an adult foster home. As of 2008, Genie was confined to a private institution for the mentally undeveloped.

One of the saddest things about this case, my student says, is that she was treated as a science experiment. Maybe if she had gotten supportive therapy, instead of being used as a test case for the latest theories. Maybe if they had just kept teaching her to speak. Maybe if she could have spoken. Maybe even just one story. Maybe. Maybe.

Page 167: *You don't get to write about me.* In *Narrative of the Life of Frederick Douglass, an American Slave,* Frederick Douglass writes about the repeated beating of his Aunt Hester. Whatever the supposed occasion—usually some order disobeyed—in every case, the master strips her nearly naked, ties her to a hook in the wall or a joist in the middle of the room, and beats her with a thick leather whip until her blood drips to the floor. There is nothing she can do or say to stop him. No prayer. No speech. No entreaty will save her. The louder she screams the harder he whips. Decades later, as he commits this memory to his autobiography, Douglass has no words to describe the feelings with which he watched this.

When Douglass is sold to Mr. and Mrs. Auld of Baltimore, his new mistress takes it upon herself to teach Douglass to read and write. Just as Douglass begins to make progress, Mr. Auld learns what is going on and forbids his wife from teaching their slave, insisting that "learning would *spoil* the best nigger in the world" (emphasis in original). If you teach slaves to read, he insists, they become unmanageable. There is no keeping them, and they grow discontented and unhappy, since education makes men forever unfit to be slaves. These words awaken Frederick Douglass to a new purpose: "From that moment, I understood the pathway from slavery to freedom."

Page 167: *There's the story I have.* See Charles M. Anderson, "Suture, Stigma, and the Pages That Heal."

Page 173: *In the story I have.* See, in particular, Georges Bataille, *Inner Experience*, and Denis Hollier, *Against Architecture: The Writings of Georges Bataille.*

Page 173: *Am I not endlessly circling?* "What did we do," asks Nietzsche's madman,

> When we detached this world from its sun? Where is it going now? Where are we going? Far from all the suns? Are we not just endlessly falling? Backward, sideways, forward, in every direction? Is there still an up and a down? Are we not being borne aimlessly into an endless void?

See "The Parable of the Madman."

Page 176: *This cave of making.* Gordon Van Ness writes in "Remembering James Dickey" (*Dos Passos* Review 2, no. 1):

> Admitted to his house, I stood waiting in the foyer while he finished typing in a room he called "the cave of making." I had seen the room once. It held a large table around which half a dozen or more typewriters sat silently waiting his attention, each holding a draft page of a project on which he was currently working. When he came out, we hugged, my arms not even coming close to encircling him while his easily wrapped around me, an unspoken camaraderie that ran deep, at what he would have called blood-level. There was conversation, good human talk on poetry and other vital subjects that mattered, not the silliness with which people in rural Southside Virginia, gathering for large swathes of time at Walmart, concern themselves—limited, and limiting, discussions of the weather, the football scores, the price of tobacco.

Page 176: *I don't know how to escape it.* In "The Silver Lily" Louise Glück writes:

> We have come too far together toward the end now
> to fear the end. These nights, I am no longer even certain
> I know what the end means. And you, who've been with
>   a man—

after the first cries,
doesn't joy, like fear, make no sound?

Secretly—I've never admitted this—I've always wanted The Man I Used to Live With to die in some sudden and tragic way (struck by lightning, hit by a train, choked on his own spit), so that I would never have to untangle these emotions, so that I could mourn him, and then move on. I've always thought there should be some easy way to just move on.

Page 176: *A trap. a puzzle. a paradox.* When speaking of paradoxes, philosophers and rhetoricians often use the term *aporia*, the English word derived from the Greek *aporos*, meaning literally "impassable" (*a*- meaning "without" and *poros* meaning "passage"): a blockage, a trap. It's the state of perplexity, of bafflement, of doubt. Derrida in particular has used the term to describe a deadlock of incompatible information—how mourning and forgiveness, for example, are made impossible by the conditions of their possibility. How possibility requires impossibility.

The opposite of *aporos*—or a puzzle, a perplexity, a paradox—is *poros*, meaning "passageway" or "opening," from which come words like the Latin *porta*, meaning "door" or "entrance" or "exit" or "escape." From *poros* come words like *port, passage, opportunity*.

These two terms, *poros* and *aporos*, the opening and the impasse, are mutually dependent: each one creates the other. An escape without a trap leads away from nowhere forever; the closure without an opening merely suspends. The *aporos* requires the *poros*. For every impasse, there must be an opening.

from thirteen

Page 181: *White of forgetfulness. White of safety.* Louise Glück, "Persephone the Wanderer."

You drift between earth and death
which seem, finally,
strangely alike. Scholars tell us

that there is no point in knowing what you want
when the forces contending over you
could kill you.

White of forgetfulness,
White of safety—

thank you

I am grateful to the editors of *Pebble Lake Review*, *TriQuarterly Online*, and *Creative Nonfiction*, where portions of this manuscript appeared over the span of many years, and in very altered form.

I am deeply grateful to my agent, Ethan Bassoff, whom I cannot thank enough for his time, energy, and tireless advocacy of this work; and to Masie Cochran, my editor at Tin House Books, whose insight and energetic vision are forces to be reckoned with. I am indebted to you both.

Thank you also to Jakob, Diane, Nanci, and the whole Tin House crew.

Thanks to the generous readers of early incarnations of this manuscript: Nick Flynn, Joshua Rivkin, Casey Fleming; and to the teachers who clarified my thinking about this book before it became one: Rubén Martínez, John Weir, Mark Doty, Claudia Rankine, Ann Christensen, J. Kastely, and W. Lawrence Hogue. Thanks also to the dedicated writers I worked alongside during this book's infancy: Elizabeth Chapman, Annie Newton, Lucy Seward, Brian Wolf, Fariha Tayaab, and Allison LiVecchi. I love you with my whole, second beating heart.

I am grateful for the generous support of the Sustainable Arts Foundation; the Millay Colony for the Arts, where a portion of this manuscript was written; and the Inprint Brown Foundation.

And finally, thank you to my husband and partner in life, whom I'll not name here, and to our children, whose love is so fierce and complete that it pulls me out of bed at night. More than anything else, I am grateful for that love.

LACY M. JOHNSON is the author of *Trespasses: A Memoir* and is coartistic director of the location-based storytelling project [the invisible city]. She lives in Houston with her husband and children.